edited by

DAVID EASTON, 1927-

Varieties of

Political Theory

PRENTICE-HALL, INC., ENGLEWOOD CLIFFS, N.J.

PRENTICE-HALL CONTEMPORARY POLITICAL THEORY SERIES

David Easton, *Editor*

PRENTICE-HALL INTERNATIONAL, INC., *London*
PRENTICE-HALL OF AUSTRALIA, PTY. LTD., *Sydney*
PRENTICE-HALL OF CANADA, LTD., *Toronto*
PRENTICE-HALL OF INDIA (PRIVATE) LTD., *New Delhi*
PRENTICE-HALL OF JAPAN, INC., *Tokyo*

Library of Congress Catalog Card Number: 66–18267

Printed in the United States of America

94064-C

Current printing (last digit):
10 9 8 7 6 5 4

Preface to
Contemporary Political Theory Series

This volume is part of a new series in political science that is devoted to empirically oriented theory. Nothing testifies more eloquently to the growing strength of empirical political theory than the conviction that now, after more than twenty-five hundred years of development, it is for the first time possible to think of building a publication series out of volumes devoted exclusively to the construction of such theory. The series is itself a sign of the times; we hope it will also provide a means for vigorously and creatively reinforcing the present tendencies.

This series will contribute to the development of contemporary political theory in several distinctive ways. First and foremost, our primary objective is to gather together brief but exciting monographs that will explore alternative approaches to empirical theory. Some of these may be concerned with general, overarching theories that seek to bring order and coherence to the whole field of political science. Others may devote themselves to less comprehensive, partial theories that help to integrate selected aspects of political life, intranational, international, and cross-national. Still others may seek to explore the theoretical assumptions of existing empirical research and to systematize and assess their findings in the hope of bringing added clarity to a subfield, enhancing its theoretical relevance, and giving it a new sense of purpose and direction. Although the main emphasis will be on stimulating the production of critical and creative works that deal with the substance of theories in such areas, on occasion it will be appropriate to include volumes that direct their attention to the methodological tasks of theory construction itself.

We expect the series to leave its impact on the development of theory in a second way. It will provide a single medium through which original monographs in empirical or descriptive theory can be assembled. We would hope thereby to stimulate and reinforce the broadest range of experimentation with respect to alternative approaches to theory. Underlying the whole series is the basic premise that only through innovative and courageous efforts in a multitude of divergent and conflicting directions will it be possible for a gradual and meaningful consensus to arise in the course of time with regard to the outlines of a useful general theory or set of partial theories. It is the very essence of the theoretical enterprise that, if and when it seems appropriate, it should feel free to sever itself from the bonds of traditional ways of looking at political life. By providing an established publishing outlet, we would hope to lend encouragement in this direction at a time when it is most needed.

Third, we would hope that the availability in a single series of a growing assemblage of volumes on empirical theory will have a decisive influence on teaching and training in this field. We are in a process of transition in political science toward a more rigorous science, and the series may be seen as another small effort to aid the change.

With regard to teaching and training in the function, tasks, and substance of empirical theory, a strong desire to improve the facilities in political science has not been wanting. But a major barrier has blocked the way. We have lacked a sufficient number of serious monographs to provide enough scope and depth to make formal courses in this area feasible as well as desirable. We would expect that in due time this series would offer a core around which courses on empirical theory might be initially developed, or where they already exist, enriched. In themselves such courses would contribute immeasurably to attracting the best minds in each generation of students to the field of theory or in sensitizing them to the actual function of theory in empirical research. By testifying to the challenge that theory presents and to the opportunities for empirical research, the series should, in its long-range effect, reinforce empirical theory as an appropriate and adventuresome area for teaching and research.

Table of Contents

INTRODUCTION

DAVID EASTON

University of Chicago

Alternative Strategies
in Theoretical Research

It has often been said that wars do not change basic intellectual or political trends, that they simply delay or modify what in any case would eventually have occurred.[1] Whether or not this is true for all wars, World War II in fact did mark a major turning point in the history of political science, one that defied recognition until a decade or more after the fact. It is true that before World War II, there were some hints of the pattern of future developments in political theory. But after 1945, a number of new currents were set in motion, the earlier detection of which would have taxed the ingenuity of even the most insightful and careful observer. Among these innovations, we find a slowly growing body of political theory unlike anything that had preceded it in the previous 2000 years.

Prior to World War II, theory almost exclusively implied moral philosophy in its various forms, or, at the very least, the history and analysis of the moral systems of the great political thinkers of the past. Only the barest glimmerings of the modern kind of theory were visible. For most students of politics, the little that did exist was scarcely recognizable as such; very seldom was it clearly identified and labelled.

---

[1] For the effects of wars on basic ideas, see J. U. Nef, *War and Human Progress* (Cambridge, Mass.: Harvard University Press, 1950).

1

Since World War II, however, there has gradually accumulated a small but distinguished inventory of this new kind of theoretical inquiry, what we may call descriptive, or empirical, theory.

Empirical theory is by no means homogeneous; it varies widely in its scope and degree of abstractness. Much of it is confined to very limited hypotheses about small fragments of political behavior; other parts of it pertain to somewhat broader ranges of political phenomena such as we find in particular sets of political institutions—in parties, administrative behavior, or electoral choices, for example. But the kind of empirical theory which represents the most striking and promising innovation since World War II seeks to illuminate the whole domain of political interaction. That is to say, the new theory which has special significance in political science seeks to systematize and lend coherence and direction to the whole field of political science as a discipline. It represents in political science what in other fields—such as economics or sociology—has been called general as against partial or special theory.[2]

Modern theory, in the form of general theory, has a number of important functions. It gives guidance to empirical research by summarizing what has been discovered and by suggesting the relevance or significance of new, proposed investigations. It acts as an economical means for storing and retrieving larger bodies of apparently discrete information about political behavior. But general theory also serves as an incentive for the creation of new information, insofar as logical operations can be performed on its theoretical propositions to extend the horizons of our understanding and explanation. In this function lies the truly creative and most rewarding potential of general theory, one that we can expect will assert itself increasingly in political science as theoretical enquiry acquires a deeper sense of security and a greater appetite for innovative boldness.

Significant as the body of modern political theory already is, it has made a mere beginning in the decades since World War II. Nevertheless, even in its paucity it represents a break with the past, the enormity of which is only slowly being absorbed into the consciousness of political scientists. We are not yet fully aware of the fact that as part of the general scientific revolution under way in the area of methods and techniques—usually described as the study of political behavior—political science is also experiencing a revolution in the field of theory that is of comparable proportions and significance.

THE IMPACT OF THE THEORETICAL REVOLUTION

The implications of this theoretical revolution are varied and profound. To appreciate fully the significance of the essays collected in this volume, it will be helpful to explore some of these implications.

[2] For extended comments on this new theory, see my *A Framework for Political Analysis* (Englewood Cliffs, N.J.: Prentice-Hall, Inc., 1965), especially Chapter One.

Theory and "the myth of methodology"

The revolution in political theory testifies to the fact that in political science we have been able to address ourselves directly to substantive construction in theory. This may seem to be a strange statement, since presumably, once we undertake to build theory, no other path would seem to be open. But the fact is that in political science we are largely unaware of the distractions and wasteful motions that we have mercifully been spared.

Unlike sociology or psychology, political science, as the doors to scientific method have finally been opened wide, has been able to avoid a long and agonizing period in which its theoretical efforts might have been buried in what has been called "the myth of methodology."[3] We have been able to take advantage of the history of other disciplines, in which all too easily theory could imperceptibly slip from substantive analysis into methodological discussion. Methodology often masqueraded under the title of theory. In exploring theoretical alternatives in political science, we have usually succeeded in distinguishing clearly between methodology and the substantive treatment of theoretical issues, assigning to each its proper place and weight.

This self-conscious awareness of the difference between substantive theory and methodological analysis has gone hand in hand with a balanced appreciation of the relative importance of rigorous fact-gathering as against theorizing. All too often, inadequate distinction between methodological discussion and theoretical analysis has been accompanied by an undue emphasis on the rigorous collection of data undirected by theoretical criteria of relevance; each reinforced the other. Preoccupation with methodology led to experimentation with varying techniques for gathering hard data; the investment of great amounts of time and labor in collecting data encouraged continued exploration of the methods used and their implications. In the period between the two World Wars, fact-gathering unregulated by theory—"hyperfactualism," as I have called it elsewhere[4]—reached its peak in the social sciences as a whole.

Although the reception of scientific method in political science did not occur until after World War II, our discipline also participated in the hyperfactualism of the 1920's and 1930's, however impressionistic our techniques were. But by the time scientific method did begin to make serious inroads into political research, after World War II, political science was spared the sins of the other social sciences. It could learn from the errors of their ways.

By the end of World War II, a new era had opened up for the other social sciences: hyperfactualism had come under sharp criticism and was already on the wane. From this new spirit, as political scientists became

[3] Abraham Kaplan, *The Conduct of Inquiry* (San Francisco: Chandler Publishing Co., 1964), p. 24.

[4] David Easton, *The Political System* (New York: Alfred A. Knopf, Inc., 1953), p. 66 ff.

increasingly hospitable to scientific method, we were quickly able to appreciate the dangers of strengthening our techniques of empirical research in the collection and interpretation of data without at the same time testing the relevance and significance of the results by reference to empirically oriented theory. The consequences of neglecting theory had become too apparent to be ignored. Thus, although in its prescientific period political science had had its own hyperfactual phase, it dropped this emphasis once it began to enter fully into its own scientific age.

Because political science has come under the full sway of scientific method as the so-called behavioral revolution has been taking hold[5] we have fortunately been able to develop the capacity to pursue a dual but parallel course. We have been successful in simultaneously sharpening our tools of empirical research and bolstering our substantive, theoretical understanding, at the highest conceptual levels. We have found it neither necessary nor desirable to substitute methodological discussion for theoretical contributions or to mistake rigorous fact-gathering for explanatory knowledge and understanding.

The bond between theory and research

The theoretical revolution in political science has had other vital implications for the place of theory in the structure of the discipline as a whole. From time immemorial, political theory has presumed to offer intellectual leadership within political science. For reasons recounted elsewhere,[6] as political science moved tentatively in the direction of a rigorous science in the first half of this century (seeking explanations rather than asserting prescriptions), the preoccupation of traditional theory with moral evaluation and with the history of ideas helped to divorce the subfield of political theory from the mainstream of research in political science as a whole. Today, however, for the first time in this century, the emergence of empirically oriented theory holds out the promise that theory can begin to reassert its intellectual leadership. Even as the techniques of rigorous research are increasingly improved and sharpened, the new political theory has defined its own tasks in such a way that it seeks to provide propositions that are ultimately testable through these very techniques. Theory seeks to march side by side with empirical research.

But of even greater significance, modern theory seeks to follow in the grand tradition of moral theory. It poses fundamental questions about the nature and direction of political enquiry, even though for modern theory this means probing deeply into the nature and direction of the new scientific

---

[5] For a full discussion of this, see David Easton, "The Current Meaning of 'Behavioralism' in Political Science," in *The Limits of Behavioralism in Political Science,* ed. J. C. Charlesworth (Philadelphia: American Academy of Political and Social Science, 1962), pp. 1–25.

[6] Easton, *The Political System.*

research as it spreads through the discipline as a whole. It is clear that modern theory has already begun to act as a major and severe solvent of the numerous unexamined assumptions prevalent in empirical research. New dimensions of political life have been uncovered; new units of analysis have been proposed; alternative over-all conceptualizations of the discipline have been invented; and new objectives for research have been suggested. Theory no longer brings up the rear, but rather seeks to act as the vanguard of research.

Modern theory as a link to the basic social sciences

From the long perspective of history, perhaps the major contribution of this theoretical revolution will prove to be its attaining for political science a permanent place in the ranks of the so-called basic social sciences. Political science has not always been accepted in this way. In the recent past, for example, other social scientists have not only entertained strong doubts about where political science stands in the social science establishment; they have at times gone so far as to construe political science as only a discipline for the application of basic knowledge acquired by the other social sciences. For them it has been an area of applied rather than of theoretical knowledge.[7]

As a result of its new theoretical tendencies, political science, for the first time, is arriving at a full appreciation of itself as a discipline with a theoretical status equivalent in every respect to those of the other social sciences. Although in the past, political science was able to define an institutional area of interest distinct from the other disciplines, it had difficulty in showing that its understanding of political phenomena possessed a theoretical coherence as isolable as political interactions themselves. Modern theory has had to do precisely that in order to establish its own validity and justify its own existence as an area of enquiry. In other words one of the major tasks of theory has been to identify a set of behaviors that it could describe as political, and, in the process, to construct an analytic system or a theory that would help to explain the behavioral reality. A political theory is but a symbolic system useful for understanding concrete or empirical political systems.

Whether or not political theory has been successful in inventing a conceptual system that explains the operations of political systems may be debatable. But what is unmistakably clear, even at this early stage in the development of modern political theory, is that political science has become aware of its own potential theoretical autonomy, that is, of a capacity for creating its own general theory applicable to the phenomena it normally

---

[7] See Talcott Parsons, *The Social System* (New York: Free Press of Glencoe, Inc., 1951), pp. 126–27; H. L. Zetterberg, *Sociology in the U.S.A.* (Paris: UNESCO, 1956), pp. 45–46.

includes within its scope. In this sense, it is a basic theoretical science equivalent in every respect to the other major social sciences.

From this conclusion, we need not of course infer that, as an area of understanding, political science stands independent of the other disciplines and can therefore explain political phenomena without reference to other major areas of behavior. The interrelatedness of behavior and of most knowledge can today be taken for granted. But the assertion that political science has become a theoretically autonomous discipline does mean that we can conceptualize the subject matter of political science so that theories of political interaction will have equal status with theories of culture, the economy, social structure, and other basic modes of social interaction.

It is no longer plausible to suggest that political science is just a field in which basic knowledge acquired in other disciplines is applied for the understanding of political institutions. Rather, through the new *optique* of empirical theory we are able to reinforce a fundamental truth: that each discipline cuts through a unique even though interrelated aspect of social life, one that is no less "fundamental" than any other aspect in the understanding of social interaction in its entirety.

The road to integration of the disciplines

A final noteworthy consequence of the theoretical revolution in political science is that it has opened the door to a new and more meaningful relationship between political science and the other disciplines. In the past, when political science enquired into the relationship between itself and the other disciplines, it was able, at the very most, to assert that it could borrow the findings and methods of the other social sciences and apply them toward a richer understanding of political phenomena. Indeed, in the older fashion, the methods of research were characteristically described as psychological, sociological, historical, and the like. In practice, little in the way of techniques was borrowed. At most, political science imported limited amounts of data and findings from the other disciplines so as to temper the assumptions upon which political interpretations proceeded. In essence, as the social sciences spun off from their parent discipline, philosophy, and as professional specialization intensified toward the end of the nineteenth century, political science, more than the other social sciences, tended to follow a separate path. It maintained its original close association with philosophy and was indifferent if not hostile to many of its neighboring disciplines. During most of the first half of the twentieth century, it almost pursued a course of splendid isolation.

But with the growth of empirical theory, political science has begun to send out new and deep roots into the other social sciences. In part, these new ties spring from the efforts of political scientists themselves to strengthen the theoretical base of their discipline.

One of the peculiar features about the development of political science, understandable because of its long connection with philosophy, is that it was unable to cultivate very much in the way of general theory from its own internal resources. We might be tempted to deny this by pointing to a single, distinguished exception—equilibrium analysis—as it emerged in the group approach to politics.[8] Even this, however, owes a great deal to sociology and its group theorists in Germany and Austria at the end of the last century, particularly as their ideas were interpreted in the United States by Albion Small and others. But aside from group analysis, which could be interpreted as more a product of pluralist philosophy than of group sociology, and therefore as a home-grown product of political science, there was very little general theorizing, of an empirical sort, within political science.

Since political science lacked a tradition from which to draw inspiration for theoretical innovation, we can appreciate why, as the scientific revolution made inroads into political science, it began to reach out to the other social sciences for help. This is particularly understandable when we look at the rapid rate of change in political science as a whole since World War II. Because of this, political science, unlike other disciplines, has lacked the time to speculate about a variety of independently generated alternatives, or to move slowly, on the basis of trial and error, toward some minimal consensus on a few selected promising approaches winnowed out of a larger body of experimentations. Rather, in retrospect, it appears that as we political scientists have searched for ways to conceptualize our discipline, we have understandably scanned the theoretical models of other scientific disciplines, natural as well as social, especially where these models helped a discipline to achieve that level of over-all self-awareness and organization expected of a maturing scientific field. If for no other reason, the combined pressures of time and necessity have imposed this strategy on us.

Through such explicit theoretical borrowing, at the very least, some interpenetration of political science with the other disciplines has begun to occur. Decision-making theories from the organizational field, the structural-functional approach from anthropology and sociology, action theory from sociology, and systems analysis from the communications sciences have offered vast reservoirs of fairly well-developed concepts and even, to a more limited extent, of theorems that have seemed cogent to students of political science.[9]

But the integration of political science with other disciplines has not been left to the initiative of political science alone. Students from the other social sciences have helped to hasten the process. And here we come upon

---

[8] See Easton, *The Political System,* Chapter Eleven.
[9] For additional comments on this, see Easton, "The Current Meaning of 'Behavioralism' in Political Science."

a phenomenon strange in the annals of science, and one that is the subject of the present volume. Social scientists outside the field of political science itself have felt impelled to invent new theoretical devices for conceptualizing politics as a whole. Without doubt, the history of the social sciences, whenever it is written, will reveal the extraordinary nature of this influx of theoretical models into political science from adjacent disciplines. Sociologists, economists, and anthropologists, among others, have turned their skills to systematizing the study of political phenomena, at a high level of theoretical generality, as the essays in this book will amply demonstrate.

There are undoubtedly many reasons why other social scientists should feel driven to do for political science what the discipline has been slow in doing for itself. Among them, the growing urgency of the political crisis in the modern world looms very large. The substitution of political for economic primacy in the United States and in most parts of the developed world could not help but impress on many social scientists the inescapable consequences of politics for all other aspects of society. In the present epoch, it has become increasingly clear among other social sciences that a minimally adequate understanding of the phenomena at the center of their own interests would be hastened if the existing knowledge of political behavior were shaped into some systematic form. Since the other social sciences had waited many decades for political science to begin to provide them with this generalized conceptualization of itself, we can appreciate why students in those disciplines should feel impatient and take matters into their own hands, even if lack of *expertise* should hamper their efforts.

Because of guild spirit in the disciplines prior to World War II, a political scientist who valued his professional honor might have cried out: "Hold! Trespassers beware! These grounds are reserved for professional political scientists alone." Although there are still some who might utter this injunction, the temper of the times has changed dramatically. We are gradually becoming accustomed to an image of ourselves as an integral part of the total scientific enterprise that pursues an understanding of man in society.

In this new spirit, since World War II many bridges have been built to link political science with the other disciplines at all levels, from the crudely empirical to the broadly theoretical. Many techniques are identical for all social science; many theorems are now shared; and even training in research overlaps. There is little of the old fear left in political science that incursions by others will result in intellectual losses. Rather, the conviction has now begun to prevail that such invasions can benefit all. There is little reason, therefore, to resist theories of politics proffered by other social scientists, simply because they bring a different kind of knowledge and *expertise* with them. This new attitude toward the increasing exchange of ideas between political science and the other social sciences receives its stimulus, then, from outside the field as well as from within.

THEORIES FROM THE OUTSIDE

These remarks bring us directly to the content of this volume of essays in political theory. As theoreticians from other disciplines have begun to bring the power of their own categories to bear upon political phenomena, we have almost imperceptibly acquired a considerable inventory of alternative strategies for the construction of general theory. Aside from any other consideration, these "external" approaches to political theory are certainly worthy of particular attention, if only because they represent the thinking of distinguished specialists in other areas. But, in addition, since these theoretical categories have a history of use in their respective disciplines, we can see them in these essays applied to political phenomena with the flexibility and sensitivity available to scholars already thoroughly at home with them in other areas.

Content of this volume

The essays in this volume are a sampling of kinds of theories that have originated outside of political science since World War II, and that are suggestive, insightful aids to the systematic organization of political knowledge. They are brought together because of the feeling that political scientists are as yet not fully aware of the extent to which adjacent disciplines have been setting political phenomena in the context of their own theories. Nor are we cognizant of the considerable variety of alternatives already at hand. And we can anticipate that this variety will continue to grow, at least until political science itself has provided more useful alternatives, not only for its own purposes but for the needs of the other disciplines as well.

In the title of this Introduction, I have called the essays in this volume "alternative strategies for theoretical research." If we wished, we might call them *theories,* as I have felt free to do as the context of this Introduction seemed to require. But we scarcely need to remind ourselves, now that empirical theory is being so thoroughly discussed in political science, that in the social sciences as a whole, theory in any ideal sense is as yet little known. It is not essential, therefore, that we accord these papers the status of theories in any rigorous sense; it is enough if we view them as programs for analysis that under appropriate conditions could develop into theories more rigorously defined.

These essays (except for my own) originated as papers for a panel at the annual meeting of the American Political Science Association in New York City, in September, 1963. As chairman of the Political Theory Section of that meeting, it occurred to me that it would be useful to bring together a few of the alternative approaches to general political theory that had been quietly evolving outside of political science. The extraordinarily large attendance at the main session of the panel devoted to these papers testified to the interest aroused by these theoretical concerns and their distinguished representatives.

Although these essays do not exhaust the possible external strategies to political analysis, they do represent most of the significant ones. The first three papers all take their point of departure from that broad area of theory that adopts decision-making or individual and social-choice processes as central concepts. Nevertheless, it is their differences that provide a focus for our interest.

For Herbert A. Simon, organizational theory provides the theoretical matrix out of which he is able to conclude that decision making is not "some highly special aspect of the political process, but . . . its central core." Although James M. Buchanan also sees the making of choices as a major phenomenon, he argues in favor of what he calls an "individualistic model," one that represents a conscious "extension of the tools, methods, and procedures utilized by the economist."

James G. March also focuses on decisions, but the emphasis of his thinking brings him to an analysis of the utility of a very old conception in political science, that of power. Although as he himself states, he feels that "the immediate implications for general theories of society . . . are probably meager," he does perhaps underestimate the significance of his own remarks. Coming at the idea of power from the general area of organizational theory, he concludes that it "gives us surprisingly little purchase in reasonable models of complex systems of social choice." Since he identifies political systems as mechanisms of social choice, the burden of the argument in his paper would eliminate power as a major dimension in the construction of a general political theory.

But, as though to illustrate the great variety in approaches to general theory, Talcott Parsons, in applying his distinguished action theory to political systems, offers an example of one way in which power can continue to be used for general theory. As in all cases where basic assumptions and theoretical premises diverge widely—organizational theory and Parsons' action theory are a good illustration—it is an interesting test of the skill of the critic to pursue the detailed kind of comparison necessary in order to evaluate the relative promise of each as a frame of reference for political analysis.

The paper by M. G. Smith represents an approach that has yet to receive the attention that it merits from political scientists. It draws directly on the so-called comparative method of anthropology to suggest an alternative strategy for general political analysis. He rejects an approach to theory based on process, content, or functions—as found, say, in action theory, related as it is to functional analysis—and opts in favor of a purely structural theory. Using Weber's type of corporation as a basic structural unit, he argues that comparison between political systems must distinguish them according to their "structural simplicity or complexity, by reference to the variety of corporate units of differing forms, bases, and functions which they contain and the principles which serve to articulate them." In effect, this paper suggests a radically new way of incorporating the badly limping "group approach" in political science into a broader theoretical structure. It may also offer political science a way of gaining maximum dividends from the great attention that political research in the past has devoted to political forms and structures.

The final essays help to shed some light on the impact of that vast and growing field of knowledge—the communication sciences—in which the dominant theoretical direction can be described as systems analysis. Anatol Rapoport draws attention to the fact that the analysis of political phenomena in these terms requires specific and detailed attention to the so-called "system properties" of political life. My own paper has been added as a concrete illustration of an introduction to one kind of systems analysis of political phenomena.

Although I have been describing the theoretical designs set forth in this volume as varieties of strategies for political theorizing derived from outside political science, it is clear that not all of the authors are formally members of other disciplines. Nevertheless, if the main inspiration of an author's theorizing or if a good part of his orientation derives from disciplines other than political science, I have taken the liberty to include his thinking in the broad category of theories originating outside political science. I have defined this category loosely since the main objective is not to impose any final label on scholars. Rather, it is to draw attention to the variety of seminal ideas in theory that are available outside the normal range of thought in political science, and that can serve to stimulate the discovery of additional patterns of analysis by political science itself.

It is not that as political scientists we are unaware of the existence of alternative strategies to theory construction. No one today in political science could be ignorant of the important role, for example, that decision making or systems analysis have begun to play in the last decade. But we see these externally initiated theories in a new and clearer light when we collect them together, recognize them as relatively well-defined alternatives, foresee their significance as a class of intellectual phenomena, and stand ready to calculate the length to which we have already gone in borrowing from them or in absorbing, into political analysis, the best of what they may have to offer.

A principle for classifying theories

It may seem somewhat strange to use as a principle of classification, "theories originating outside political science," as contrasted with those emerging from thought patterns that have evolved largely within political science. The forthright simplicity of this principle of classification, however, is no accident.

There are many other useful ways of classifying theories. We might divide them according to their scope—whether they are micro- or macro-theories; according to their function—whether they seek to deal with statics or dynamics, with structure or process, or with individual, isolated political systems or systems comparatively considered; according to their structure—whether they are postulational systems of thought with closely knit, logical interrelatedness or whether they constitute a more loosely defined set of propositions; or according to their level—by the relationship of the behavioral systems to which they refer as ranked on some hierarchical scale.

Each classification needs to be assessed according to the purposes for which it is used. Here I have chosen disciplinary affinity or source of a theory, separating those outside political science from those within it. Several reasons support the utility of this division.

In the first place, by implication it illuminates the process of theory formation itself. It shows that the theoretical imagination does not need to wait for spontaneous generation to occur within a discipline. Theoretical ideas are hard enough to come by, and there is nothing in the nature of theory that forbids borrowing and adaptation on as large a scale as seems necessary and feasible.

In the second place, the paternity of a theory helps us to understand its strengths, limits, and implications. Whatever weaknesses a theory might have on its home grounds can be expected to infect the theory as it is elaborated for use in understanding political phenomena. The disciplinary affinity of a theory, therefore, is of crucial importance in alerting us to its full implications.

Finally, the fact of borrowing itself reveals to us the full measure and meaning of the theoretical revolution in political science. It demonstrates that the disciplines reach out to each other at the most general level of abstraction, and that this is one of the central mechanisms for intellectual exchanges in any age of specialization. Therein lies a major potential source of convergence if not of unity in the perspectives of the various social sciences.

This thought merits further exploration. It has frequently been observed that the unity of science cannot lie in its subject matter. Each of the major sets of disciplines—the physical, biological, and social—addresses itself to different kinds of data. And within these sets of data, each individual discipline distinguishes itself from the others by its different kind of subject matter. Only the most unrelenting kind of reductionism, such as extreme atomic physicalism, could argue for the fundamental unity of the subject matter of all science, whether natural or social.

If we accept without further argument that the similarity of all the sciences cannot lie in the commonality of the subject matter that they study, method alone remains as a possible major source of unity. That is to say, we are able to attribute the quality "scientific" to all of the sciences because they all adhere to scientific method even though they may apply it through the use of different specific techniques. In method lies the basic unity of all science. This conclusion has been long accepted in the philosophy of science.

But when we become alert to the range of alternative models lying outside of political science, models that seek to seduce political scientists to adopt their different ways of perceiving the problems of general political analysis, we are forcibly awakened to another unifying force actively at work in the history of all science, social as well as natural. It opens up the possibility that we no longer need to attribute the unity of all science to method alone. It is likely that through borrowing theories from each other, the sciences have all been able to maintain some minimal connection, if not cohesion, even in the face of their diverse subject matters and the centrifugal tendencies of specialization. Herein lies a neglected force working toward the unity of the disciplines.

In looking at the relationship between political science and relevant theories external to it, we are reminded that in every age there have been dominant theoretical patterns that have filtered into all of the basic areas of knowledge. But these patterns become dominant, not through any mystical, ethereal force but because they are in fact borrowed by one discipline from another and adapted to the needs of the host. For centuries, Newtonian mechanics endured as the theoretical model for the social as well as for the natural sciences. Darwin's evolutionary theories permeated all realms of thought in the last half of the nineteenth century. Similarly today, cybernetics—the science of communication and control—or in its broader conception, systems analysis, has spread into all corners of intellectual endeavor.

We may therefore view stimulation from outside of a discipline as one major mechanism in the diffusion of theoretical patterns. By virtue of this, external theoretical stimulation also takes its place as a vital means for holding the whole scientific intellectual enterprise together in some kind of minimal unified framework.

Thus, in looking at conceptualizations of politics as they appear in other disciplines, we are at the very least enhancing our understanding of the way in which political science, through its theoretical revolution, is becoming part of the larger enterprise that is science today. This in itself is one major ground for classifying theories in the way we have. But in addition, this approach enables us to take advantage of our knowledge about the way in which theory tends to spill over the disciplines, regardless of formal boundaries and specialties. Insofar as we are able to raise this process to a higher level of consciousness, we shall be better able to test the relevance of major theoretical ideas permeating an age, regardless of their origin, for an understanding of the fundamental problems of politics.

ONE

HERBERT A. SIMON

Carnegie Institute of Technology

Political Research:
The Decision-Making Framework

In identifying "approaches" to political research, one should not regard the various particular approaches as mutually exclusive, much less as antithetical. Reification of catchy phrases leads only to sterile methodological dispute. If I had used the labels "action theory," "game theory," "economic theory," or "influence theory" for what I am about to say, my comments would not be much altered. The comments will be more relevant for showing what different frameworks have in common than for distinguishing them.

In talking about decision making, I am dealing not with some highly special aspect of the political process, but with its central core. Voting, legislating, adjudicating, and administering have always been conceived of as decision-making processes. The tools of political analysis—legal, historical, and behavioral—have always been adapted to the analysis of decision. The use of a decision-making framework for political research is not novel; rather, it represents continuing development along paths that stretch back to the beginnings of political science.

EXPLANATION OF DECISION MAKING

What does it mean to "explain" decision-making behavior? What questions are we asking of the phenomena, and what would we accept as an answer? There is no single or simple meaning for the term *explanation*. Thus, I shall take a particular, rather than a general, point of view that has proved especially fruitful in the analysis of decision making. Let me introduce it by way of two rather different examples.

First, consider a succession of polls taken of a panel of citizens during an election campaign, or even during a series of campaigns. In the initial poll, the respondents may be asked a number of questions whose answers will help to "place" them in the social system according to age, sex, occupation, income, education, race, religion, and national and ethnic origin. They may also be asked about previous political behavior and previous and current attitudes on issues and candidates. In each successive poll, they may be asked about their preferences among candidates or their voting intentions, and about their attitudes on issues. They may also be asked about their patterns of political communication: their exposure to such communication and their initiation of political activity. Few voting studies have been as comprehensive as the one I am describing, which may perhaps be an ideal type. Still, some recent studies have approached this ideal.[1]

Whatever the comprehensiveness of the sequence of polls, I am concerned with the questions we would like to answer with its aid. I submit that we would regard the phenomena as "explained" if we could state a relatively simple set of invariant rules or "laws" that would enable us to predict the answers to all the questions in the poll at time t on the basis of our knowledge of the answers to the questions on the polls prior to time t, and correspondingly, predict the actual voting, communication, or other political behavior of the respondents at time t on the basis of the information gathered prior to time t.[2]

In other words, we want a valid dynamic theory, with *dynamic* meaning exactly what it means in the field of mechanics. This is not a vacuous specification, for the laws of dynamics have a specific form. They do not simply state how the world is at any given time; they state a relation between the way the world is at some initial time, say t_0, and the way it is at some later time, say t_1. Thus, the Newtonian laws enable us to predict where the planets will be only if we know where they are and have been. Specifically, by telling us what the accelerations will be as functions of the current positions of the parts of the system, the laws enable us to calculate the future positions from the current accelerations and velocities.

Not all physical laws are laws of dynamics. For example, in a mechanical system at rest on the earth, the center of gravity assumes the lowest position compatible with the system's freedom of motion. This is a statement of how the world is at any time when it is in static equilibrium—the position of equilibrium is independent (at least wherever this law holds) of the pre-

[1] B. R. Berelson, P. F. Lazarsfeld, and W. N. McPhee, *Voting* (Chicago: University of Chicago Press, 1954).
[2] Berelson, *et al., Voting,* pp. 280–86.

vious history of the system. Most physical laws, however, are dynamic laws, and most static laws are special cases—equilibrium cases—of more general dynamic laws.

This state of affairs—the predominance of dynamics—is not a matter of aesthetic preference among scientists. Indeed, it would be much simpler for all concerned if nature could be explained statically. The Greeks had a go at it: Things behave according to their natures; light bodies rise, heavy ones fall, everything seeks its appropriate place in the world. The only difficulty was that the explanation didn't work—hence Galileo and Newton. The simplest invariant laws that actually accounted for the observable phenomena were found to be dynamic laws, differential equations, instead of static laws.

The task, then, is to state laws of voting behavior in dynamic form: to explain the vote or voting intention at time t_1 as a (simple) function of the state of the respondent at time t_0 and the events impinging upon him between t_0 and t_1. There are already, of course, a number of theoretical models that have just this structure: the Markoff chain models and related schemes devised by T. W. Anderson, James Coleman, and William McPhee, researchers associated with the Bureau of Applied Social Research at Columbia University. For the moment, their models will serve as examples of the kind of explanatory scheme I have in mind.[3]

My second example concerns a sequence of foreign policy decisions —the decisions in the Quemoy crisis, that have been analyzed by C. A. McClelland.[4] Here again it appears unpromising to seek simple invariant principles that will predict "what the actors will decide." It is much less unrealistic to suppose that we can find simple invariant *relational* principles that will predict the actors' *next* decisions as a function of the situation as it has developed up to the given moment. Thus, McClelland identifies four major occasions of decision in the Quemoy crisis, each occasion defined by the situation that had been created by the previous decisions (of both parties) and by events.

Again, dynamic models for situations of this kind have more than once been constructed. In the foreign policy area, we can go all the way back to Richardson's classic and pioneering mathematical model of an armaments race.[5] I have selected the microstructure of the Quemoy crisis rather than

[3] See, for example, T. W. Anderson, "Probability Models for Analyzing Time Changes in Attitudes," in *Mathematical Thinking in the Social Sciences*, ed. P. F. Lazarsfeld (New York: Free Press of Glencoe, Inc., 1954); W. N. McPhee, *Formal Theories of Mass Behavior* (New York: Free Press of Glencoe, Inc., 1963); J. S. Coleman, *Introduction to Mathematical Sociology* (New York: Free Press of Glencoe, Inc., 1964).

[4] C. A. McClelland, "Decisional Opportunity and Political Controversy: The Quemoy Case," *The Journal of Conflict Resolution*, VI (September, 1962), 201–13.

[5] See L. W. Richardson, *Arms and Insecurity* (Chicago: Quadrangle Books, 1961).

the macrostructure of an armaments race as my example to emphasize that the construction of dynamic theories is not limited to situations that are easily quantified or mathematized in a classical sense. In the case of the armaments race, or of the formal dynamic models of voting behavior, the behavior to be explained is described in terms of a relatively few dimensions and variables in those dimensions that can be quantified. It is not immediately obvious how to formalize the Quemoy case in a comparable way. Moreover, most of the political phenomena that interest us do not appear amenable to quantification.

Nothing I have said about the distinction between dynamic and static theories implies quantification, however. I have simply observed that the invariants of nature may often not be absolute invariants—in the sense of rules about how the world is—but rather relative invariants—relations between how the world is at one time and at a slightly later time. Whether we are seeking quantitative or qualitative explanation, we must decide which kinds of invariants we are seeking. And in the long run, of course, our choice must be governed not by our preference but by our success in actually discovering invariant laws of one or the other kind.

Furthermore, if we are to deal adequately with the qualitative richness of history, as exemplified by the Quemoy case or by a sequence of constitutional decisions, we shall need to find formal languages for stating dynamic laws that go far beyond the resources of the languages of classical mathematics. As I shall explain presently, I think we now have such languages.

PHASES IN DECISION MAKING

I have been speaking as though decision making were synonymous with the whole stream of action. Whether or not this is true depends, of course, on how broadly we construe the term *decision making*. I have been construing it very broadly; not all contemporary theories of decision do. There has grown up in economics and mathematical statistics in the last generation—and by now it is familiar to almost all the social sciences—*mathematical decision theory,* which deals with something far more restricted than what I have been calling the decision-making process.

In this narrower sense, decision theory is concerned with the selection of an optimal course of action from among a set of specified alternative courses of action, on the basis of a criterion of preference. The theory has reached a high level of formal elegance, and has been applied, to good effect, to a number of explanatory tasks—but more especially to a number of normative ones—in the social sciences. Clearly, decision theory, thus limited, is not a theory of the stream of human individual or social behavior.[6]

[6] On the relation of the decision-making process as discussed here to formal decision theory, see my *Administrative Behavior,* 2nd ed. (New York: The Macmillan Company, 1957), pp. xxvii–xxix; and my *Models of Man* (New York: John Wiley & Sons, Inc., 1957), pp. 196–206.

If we examine such a stream of behavior, we find that much of it is concerned with determining which decision problems shall be attended to. Other parts of it are concerned with discovering or designing possible courses of action. Only a small part of it—in man-hour terms—is concerned with selecting a particular course of action, on the basis of a well-defined criterion of choice, from a set of alternatives already specified. The dynamic theory we are seeking will necessarily be a theory of the whole spectrum of decision-making activity—attention directing, design, and choice—and not just a theory of one segment.[7]

This conclusion is itself a fundamental and very significant empirical generalization about human behavior. It would not hold true in all imaginable worlds. In particular, it would not hold true in a world so simple and constrained that all the alternatives of action could be enumerated, once and for all, and could be evaluated in terms of some definite criterion of choice. In such a world, attention directing would be absent, for everything relevant could be attended to; alternative design would be absent, for all alternatives would be known at the outset; only choice would remain. Formal decision theory, as it has been developed, might explain behavior in that world excellently.

Alas, that world is not our world. Our world is a world of limited, serial information processors dealing with complexity that, for all practical purposes, is infinite in comparison with their information-gathering and computing powers. It is a world peopled by creatures of bounded rationality. Because we cannot simultaneously attend to everything that is potentially relevant, we must have processes that determine the focus of attention. If alternatives are not given but must be discovered, then there must be processes for seeking them out. The actual choice among alternatives may well turn out to be relatively inconsequential in comparison with the processes that determine what alternatives are available for choice.

Hence, to account for decisions in 1963 in the field of civil rights, one must do more than explain the committee or floor votes on proposed amendments to the civil rights bill, or on the bill itself. He will also have to explain, first of all, how civil rights came to be on the agenda at all, and close to the top of that agenda, in 1963. How did attention come to focus on that issue instead of on all the other issues that might stir men?

Second, to explain the civil rights decisions, one will have to explain how particular proposed courses of action came into being. Sit-in demonstrations, for example, only became common in 1961 or 1962. To be sure, the sit-in was not a new invention—it was a simple adaptation of the sit-down strikes of the 1930's. But how did it become an alternative to be considered by the civil rights advocates? One could argue that the sit-in alternative was "really there" before 1961 in some implicit or potential

7 See "The Executive as Decision Maker," in H. A. Simon, *The Shape of Automation* (New York: Harper & Row, Publishers, Inc., 1965), pp. 53–61.

sense, but was tacitly rejected as the preferred course of action. But, although such an argument would save the formalism of optimal decision theory, it would clash with the psychological facts.

Many other examples of the invention or design of alternative courses of action could be cited. The Peace Corps, for instance, is best understood as such an invention, devised to symbolize the program of the New Frontier. Although, like all inventions, it had its precursors—in this case, one clear precursor was the Civilian Conservation Corps—the Peace Corps existed as an alternative of action only after the idea of it had been conceived and developed.[8]

Nor are political parties and political candidates always to be regarded as "pre-existing" alternatives. To be sure, an election can usually be analyzed, in the short run, as a choice by voters among a given set of parties and candidates. But a longer-run explanation of the dynamic unrolling of events must account also for the parties and candidates themselves. An adequate science of political behavior would explain the "invention" and rise of the Republican party in the 1850's and the four-party choice of 1948. It would account not only for choices among candidates, but also for the "availability" of particular men as candidates. When the first draft of this essay was written, four men appeared likely as the 1964 Republican candidate: Goldwater, Rockefeller, Romney, and Scranton. There are perhaps 20 million adult male Republicans. Why these four? I am not suggesting that the phenomenon is mysterious, but merely that it is one of the phenomena that theory must explain.

Similar comments can be made about the determinants of the focus of attention. Individual human beings are constructed basically as serial information-processing machines. They can attend to only one, or to a few, things at a time. This fundamental fact has wide-ranging consequences for behavior.

The body politic is composed of a very large number of human beings. Hence, it is perfectly capable of operating as a parallel system, carrying on many activities simultaneously. Schools do not have to be suspended or factories closed while a fire is extinguished (unless the fire is very large or the community very small). Nevertheless, some crucial political processes—in particular, legislative and institutional changes that affect important, conflicting values—occur only in the presence of the simultaneous attention of large numbers of citizens. If one such issue is on the active agenda, most others are crowded off. A simple example of this is the postponement, by

[8] Surprisingly little systematic attention has been paid to attention-directing and alternative-generating processes in politics. For a development of some of these points, see "How Governmental Organizations Originate," in H. A. Simon, D. W. Smithburg, and V. A. Thompson, *Public Administration* (New York: Alfred A. Knopf, Inc., 1950), pp. 25–54. See also R. A. Bauer, Ithiel Pool, and L. A. Dexter, *American Business and Public Policy* (New York: Atherton Press, 1963).

mutual consent, of most consideration of vital domestic issues during war-time. One reason, of course, for the attention bottleneck is that most important changes call for action by the President and Congress, or other specific, unique institutions. Congress does have a capacity for parallel action through its committee system, but that capacity is modest, and applies largely to routine, low-temperature matters. Moreover, the formal and informal communication channels of the society appear to be capable of handling only a very few topics at any given time. The notion of "focus of public attention" could be readily operationalized by a content analysis of barbershop conversations or a line count of newspaper stories.

The theory of political behavior is concerned, then, with three aspects of the decision-making process. It must expound the rules that govern the shift and persistence of attention on the particular issues that occupy the political arena. It must state the principles that govern the invention or design of potential courses of political action. And it must set forth the conditions that determine which actions will be chosen. In all three spheres of explanation, we may expect the laws to take the form of dynamic principles: expressing relations between the state of affairs at any particular moment in time, and the events that can be expected to follow shortly thereafter.

THE LANGUAGE OF DECISION-MAKING THEORY

How sanguine we are about our prospects for determining these laws depends on our assessment of the techniques available for stating and testing theory. In this respect, we are infinitely better off today than we were a decade ago.

Dynamic theories in the physical sciences take the form of systems of differential equations, which provide rules for the change in the system through the next short interval of time as a function of the present position of the system. The rules are themselves invariant. But since the invariance they state is a *relation* between present situation and change in the system, the behavior they predict can have the greatest variety.

The difficulty in using differential equations as the language of theory in political science has come in describing the system we are concerned with in terms of a few variables of the kind familiar to classical mathematics. In some cases, there are quite natural ways of doing this—the percentage of Republican votes in a particular election, or the size of a nation's annual armaments expenditure are variables already stated in the required form. But most cases are not so amenable.

In treating the Quemoy crisis, for example, how shall we characterize as a variable the American position at any given point in time? The traditional answer to this kind of problem has been to construct scales. Thus, we might construct a sequence of possible American positions, and scale them according to degree of restraint or aggressiveness. Scales need not be one-dimensional; and the number of dimensions needed to characterize a set of alternatives can often be established operationally.

Nevertheless, when we characterize the qualitative richness of the actual phenomena by scaling, we must discard a great deal of information—perhaps most of the information that is present. A more direct method for handling streams of symbol emissions (for most social behavior is just that) would be highly desirable. Such a method is now available. The modern digital computer will in fact emit and respond to sequences of symbols. Its capacity to do so is quite general and flexible, its pattern of emission and response being determined by a stored program.

At a formal level, the program of a computer is the counterpart of a set of differential equations. It is a set of invariant rules that specifies the behavior of the computer during the next interval of time as a function of the state of the computer (its memory content and the incoming stream of symbols) at the present instant. Hence, a computer program can serve as a theory for a dynamic system. Programs can be written that are precisely equivalent to any classical system of differential equations, describing a numerical system. Hence, a computer can be programmed to simulate the equations of Richardson's armament race theory, or of a dynamic theory of voting preference.[9]

But one can also write computer programs that state nonnumerical theories about the symbol-processing systems. The symbols read and emitted by a computer do not have to represent numbers; they can equally well represent the letters of the alphabet or, for that matter, words. Thus, we might hope to construct a theory of the Quemoy crisis that, given an appropriate description of the initial situation, would actually predict the actions and policy pronouncements of the contending parties. One part of this program would be a theory of the decision-making process of the American government; another, a theory of the decision-making process of the Chinese government. Each of these theories would incorporate the decision premises of the government, and a set of processes for making decisions on the basis of these premises. The processes of the two governments might or might not resemble each other; that would have to be determined on the basis of the empirical evidence.

This kind of theory building is not chimerical. Comparable theories have already been built and partially tested for decision-making situations that are at most an order of magnitude or two simpler than this one.[10] Clarkson has built a theory, in the form of a computer program, of the

[9] The use of computer programs as theories is discussed at some length in Allen Newell and H. A. Simon, "Computers in Psychology," in *Handbook of Mathematical Psychology*, eds. R. D. Luce, R. R. Bush, and Eugene Galanter (New York: John Wiley & Sons, Inc., 1963).

[10] For a nontechnical description of these programs, see Newell and Simon, "Computers in Psychology, or *Shape of Automation*, pp. 76–92.

decision-making processes of a bank-trust investment officer.[11] Cyert and March have simulated a department-store buyer.[12] Newell, Shaw, and I have built a theory of the processes of laboratory subjects solving simple problems,[13] and a theory, much less veridical in its present form, of the decision-making processes of a chess player.[14] What these programs show in general is that the range of things a human being takes into account when he is making a complex decision is not enormous, and that the thought processes he goes through are not terribly involved or sophisticated. There is no reason why, even with existing computing equipment, we should not aspire to write programs to simulate the decision-making processes of a voter, a Congressman, or an administrator. Our first attempt will probably not be very accurate, but the point is that we have the technical means for constructing such theories, and the means, through simulation, for testing them.

But what can we learn by constructing theories in the form of computer programs that we cannot learn by common sense? I think you will find the answer most clearly by harking back to your high-school algebra and your first encounters with simultaneous equations. How were you able to solve problems, using simultaneous equations, that you could not solve without them? The trick is that with algebra as a tool, you do not initially have to deal with the problem as a whole, but only with its separate parts or mechanisms. Each individual problem statement gets translated into a single algebraic statement. When all of these have been written down, the machinery of algebra—the algorithm for solving simultaneous equations—does the rest of the work. *It* calculates the consequences of the interactions among the individual mechanisms you have specified, and traces out these interactions where the human mind, unaided, would quickly become lost.

Similarly, in constructing programs as theories of human decision-making processes, we begin by postulating simple mechanisms as the basis for the system. We then test whether the apparently complex behavior of the system as a whole may not be the inevitable outcome of the interactions of these simple mechanisms. In this way, the processes of selective search, of abstraction, and even of intuition that characterize human problem-solving activity have been produced from a relatively simple set of symbol-manipulating processes for carrying out means–end analysis. There is every reason to think that these and other equally simple processes can account for many of the phenomena of political decision making.

[11] G. P. E. Clarkson, *Portfolio Selection: A Simulation of Trust Investment* (Englewood Cliffs, N.J.: Prentice-Hall, Inc., 1962).

[12] R. M. Cyert and J. G. March, *A Behavioral Theory of the Firm* (Englewood Cliffs, N.J.: Prentice-Hall, Inc., 1963), pp. 128–48.

[13] For a brief description and further references, see Newell and Simon, "Computers in Psychology," and *The Shape of Automation*, pp. 82–86.

[14] Allen Newell, J. C. Shaw, and H. A. Simon, "Chess-Playing Programs and the Problem of Complexity," *IBM Journal of Research and Development*, II (1958), 320–35.

CONCLUSION: THE DECISION-MAKING FRAMEWORK

I have argued that the regularities of political phenomena that we are seeking through our research are likely to take predominately the form of dynamic laws—laws that state an invariant relation between present state and change in a system. For a system of human behavior, these laws must explain the focus of attention, the search for alternatives of action, and the choice among alternatives.

Over the past twenty-five years, empirical research and theory building have made substantial progress along these lines. Progress is now being greatly accelerated by the use of the digital computer as a new instrument for stating and testing theories. By stating our theories of human decision making in the form of computer programs for nonnumerical symbol manipulation, we relieve ourselves of the difficult task of "mathematizing" the theory in order to formalize it. And by using the computer as a device to simulate the behavior of the system thus programmed, we have a powerful means for inferring the consequences of the interactions of the simple mechanisms we have postulated in the program, and for comparing these consequences with actual streams of human behavior.

TWO

JAMES M. BUCHANAN

University of Virginia

An Individualistic Theory
of Political Process

The "theory" or "approach" presented in this paper represents an extension of the tools, methods, and procedures utilized by the economist to an analysis of politics. Like the political scientist, the economist studies social organization. But the economist does so, or should do so, differently. He studies the emergence of market and exchange relationships out of the choice processes of individual participants. Orthodox neoclassical economic theory gives a central position to the theory of individual choice behavior; and the textbooks normally begin with an analysis of individual demand for goods and services. Upon this theory of individual choice behavior, a theory of interaction among individuals and groups is constructed. The organization that comes into being as a result of individuals participating variously in exchange processes is called "the economy." This organization, this economy, as such, has no independent existence apart from the interaction of individual participants in it. It has no goals, no purposive intent.[1] It is prop-

---

[1] As Gunnar Myrdal pointed out in his fundamental methodological critique, many economists have erred in inferring "social" content in the results of the market economy, without making explicit value statements. See *The Political Element in the Development of Economic Theory* (London: Routledge and Kegan Paul, Ltd., 1953).

erly a social organization, but it is not a social organism. The word *individ-ualistic* in the title of this paper is the opposite of the word *organismic,* and it classifies the approach taken in terms of methodology, not in terms of ideology.

In the individualistic approach, the polity is examined as a social or-ganization in a manner similar to that in which the economy has tradition-ally been analyzed. The political structure is conceived as something that *emerges* from the choice processes of individual participants. This approach to politics is not, of course, novel. The whole of the contractarian tradition can, in one sense, be classified as falling within this approach. It nevertheless seems to be true that individual behavior in participating in and in determin-ing the outcome of political process has been relatively neglected by politi-cal scientists. Many of these scholars continue to assume that, somehow and somewhere, there exists a "public interest" or "general interest" that is di-vorced from the interests of the individual participants. In their behavior in the economic process, private people, as consumers, workers, investors, and entrepreneurs, are assumed to have differing tastes, desires, and values. And the economy represents the institutional or organizational response to the need to satisfy simultaneously this manifold set of wants. By contrast, and with important exceptions, when individuals participate in the formation of social or collective decisions, they are assumed to be somehow identical. Political process has not been sufficiently examined as a means through which separate and differing individual and group interests come to be rec-onciled, although major contributions have been made in this country by the so-called Bentley school.

This school aside, political process has continued to be viewed as a means through which "right" or "correct" decisions are reached. Political decisions are, for the most part, still conceived as "truth judgments"; the primary task of political decision making becomes that of discovering the "true" public interest. When collective choices reduce to mutually exclu-sive, either-or, decisions, this "truth judgment" model has some validity. The basic issue is whether or not it is the appropriate model for analyzing the ordinary day-to-day operation of a democratic political structure. The approach to be developed here is based on the presumption that it is not, and that the political process in democratic society can best be examined by interpreting it as a means of reconciling divergent interests. The theory is one of "individualist democracy" as opposed to "idealist democracy," in the terms used by T. D. Weldon.[2]

The acceptance of this individualistic model as the appropriate one for analysis involves value judgment in two separate respects. As one who ac-cepts the traditions of Western society, I think that we should treat the

[2] T. D. Weldon, *States and Morals* (New York: McGraw-Hill Book Com-pany, 1947).

human individual as the basic philosophical entity, and that we should conceive the state as if it were ultimately derivative from individual consent. The second value judgment, which is more important for the purposes of this paper, is a judgment about facts, a "characterizing value judgment," to use Nagel's term; it may be accepted independently of any judgment concerning the philosophy of the state. It involves the empirical judgment that political process can be "factored down" to the level of individual choices.

This statement need not, of course, involve the claim of exclusive, or even predominant, relevance for the individualistic model in making predictions about political decision processes. In the scientific house there are many mansions, and, in analyzing politics, there is surely room for alternative models. For some purposes, an organic model may be helpful; for others, a ruling-class or force theory of the state. And, in many instances, a model that bypasses the individual and begins with the interplay of group interests may yield fully satisfactory predictions. As base, it is claimed only that the model which derives the whole political process from the decisions made by individual persons, who are assumed to behave rationally, explains elements of politics that seem awkward in other models, by providing some "explanations" of reality that are not consistent with alternative theories.

At this point, a familiar methodological difficulty arises, one that caused a certain ambivalence in the more extensive treatment of this approach to politics that Gordon Tullock and I have published.[3] What is required of a "theory" of politics? There are two possible answers to this question. "Theory" may, first of all, be conceived of as a logical structure, an "explanation," which allows meaningful statements to be made and which helps to establish some uniformity in thinking without producing conceptually refutable hypotheses. At this level, which may be called that of "logical theory," all that is required in the individualistic model is that interests differ, and that individuals act in accordance with these separate interests. There is no need to examine the nature of these differences in individual and group wants. All that is required for the formal structure of a theory is the presumption that different individuals want to accomplish different things through the political mechanism. This "logical theory" of individualist democracy can be helpful in understanding the processes through which persons and groups compromise and reconcile their differences in a system of political order.

For a genuinely predictive theory of politics, however, more is needed. If by "theory" we mean the development of hypotheses about behavior in the political process that can be conceptually refuted by observation of real-world events, some additional constraints must be placed

[3] *The Calculus of Consent: Logical Foundations of Constitutional Democracy* (Ann Arbor: University of Michigan Press, 1962).

on the manner in which separate interests differ. The most familiar of these constraints, again taken from economics, is the hypothesis that individuals act in politics as they are assumed to act in the predictive theory of markets, so as to maximize their expected utility, and that their behavior in doing so is measurable in terms of some objectively identifiable magnitude such as personal income or wealth. In politics, this "positive" theory implies that individuals, and groups, act so as to further their economic positions. For example, California farmers vote for Congressmen who vote for Federal funds for irrigation projects; and owners of trucking firms vote for Congressmen who vote for highway expenditure projects. Clearly, this hypothesis has at least *some* explanatory value. Alternative constraints on the pattern of individual differences could, of course, be imposed; hypotheses could be drawn, and the implications tested.

It should be emphasized that the acceptance of the individualistic approach to politics need not imply acceptance of the hypothesis that men and groups, even in a first approximation, act narrowly to further identifiable self-interest. As a logical theory of political behavior, the model is equally applicable to a world of altruists and to a world egoists, although the testable hypotheses would of course sharply differ in the two cases. The logical construction can be applied even to a world of saints, so long as their separate visions of the "good society" differ. The model is inapplicable only to a world where separate individual interests really do not exist, but, instead, are somehow transcended in some supraindividual set of goals.

What contribution can the individualistic approach make to an understanding of politics? The underlying proposition is that individual interests differ. Starting from this, what happens to the "public interest?" Does it exist, and, if it does, how can individual interests be reconciled with it? The standard approach in political science seems to have been that of beginning with the "public interest," defined perhaps in terms of what the modern welfare economists refer to as a "social welfare function." The whole problem of "politics and morals," of "political obligation" arises out of attempts to get people to accept the "public interest" as their own. In other words, the reconciliation, if there is any, between private and public interests, must come about through some moral force that the latter exerts on individual behavior. Political behavior of the individual becomes, in this familiar approach, necessarily moral behavior.

This whole conception of politics is foreign to the approach that is summarized in this paper. There exists no "social welfare function," no "public interest" as such in a society of freely choosing individuals, and there seems no reason to invent such a conception for analytical convenience. This does not imply, however, that political process reduces to a simple struggle for power among individuals and groups, which may be analyzed systematically and scientifically, but about which nothing can be said normatively. It is precisely at this stage that the individualistic model can rescue the "public interest," indirectly, through the essential separation between the constitutional and the operational stages of political decision. The clarification of this separation, and the implications that may be derived from an understanding of it, is the central contribution that the model can make to political theory.

It is necessary to distinguish sharply between day-to-day political decision making, where the struggle often does reduce simply to that among conflicting individual-group interests, and "constitutional" decision making, where individuals may be thought of as participating in choices on the set of rules under which subsequent day-to-day decisions are to be made. This second set of decisions, of choices, which may be called the "constitutional," is the important one, and, at this stage, it becomes possible to reconcile separate individual interests with something that could, with some legitimacy, be called the "public interest" were it not for the confusion that this particular usage might generate.

The center of attention becomes the mental calculus of the individual as he is confronted with a choice among alternative rules for the reaching of subsequent political decisions—that is to say, as he is confronted with a genuinely constitutional issue. The individual does not know, nor is he able to predict, what particular issues will be presented subsequent to the adoption of the rule. And, even if he can predict with some accuracy the sort of issues that may arise, he could hardly predict his own position vis-à-vis the other members of the group. Faced with such uncertainty, how does he proceed to choose among alternative rules? He must, in the nature of the case, try to select a rule that will work reasonably well for an unpredictable series of events and in terms of his own personal situation that he will assume to be more or less randomly distributed. Simple self-interest dictates that the individual try to rank alternative rules and institutions for collective decision making. The essential element here is the recognition that self-interest, at the level of decisions on rules or on institutions that are expected to remain in effect for long time periods, imposes on the individual an attitude and a behavior pattern that are not identical with those which the same self-interest would dictate in particular choices on specific political issues.

The members of the group may, of course, disagree on the rules, as they discuss these at the constitutional level of decision. A consensus on the ranking of alternative institutional schemes will not necessarily emerge. But it is precisely at this constitutional stage that discussion in some meaningful sense can take place. It is at this stage where analysis and argument can be helpful in resolving differences of opinion. No moral issue is introduced in this procedure; there is no dilemma that requires the individual to choose between furtherance of his own self-interest, as he perceives it, and some vague "public interest" as sensed by others than himself, with a view toward preserving social harmony. The reconciliation that is possible here is achieved through the fact that self-interest, as the individual himself perceives this, becomes less and less identifiable in any objectively measurable sense, for the individual is removed from the moment of pure conflict.

The analogy with the choosing of rules for an ordinary game is helpful, as my colleague, Rutledge Vining, has repeatedly emphasized. Consider the individual who participates in a poker game at the start of an evening's play. Rules under which play is to proceed are discussed and debated. There is no departure from pure self-interest required for the individual to choose rules that will, in fact, be predicted to result in a reasonably "fair" game. Not knowing in advance how the cards will be distributed over a whole series of particular plays, the participant will, in his own interest, be motivated to choose rules that will make the game "fair," that is, "in the general interest of the group." Various players or prospective players may, of course, disagree on the precise content of the rules that are required to produce "fair" games. But these differences will be based, not so much on differences in identifiable self-interest, but on differences in characterizing value judgments concerning the working properties of alternative rules, that is to say, concerning the frequency distribution of predicted outcomes. Ultimate agreement may not be possible, and the game may not be played. But it seems that genuine compromise, genuine consensus, is much more likely to result in this sort of situation than at that stage where, by necessity and invention, individual positions come to be directly opposed, one to the other.

At the constitutional level of discourse, unanimity or consensus becomes important, not because there is something sacrosanct about unanimity per se, but for the simple reason that it provides the *only* criterion through which improvements in rules and institutions can, in fact, be judged without the introduction of an explicit value scale. Lacking an explicit social welfare function, there is no external or exogenous means of evaluating possible changes in the rules or institutions that describe an existing political structure. And, if agreement on possible changes in these cannot be secured, how are the interests of the separate individuals or groups to be weighed, one against the other? Agreement becomes the only possible test, and if this does not, or cannot, exist, there is simply nothing that can be said. Disagreement precludes any conclusion. But it should be again emphasized that the standard arguments against the application of the unanimity rule do not apply with equal force at the constitutional level and at the operational level of choice. Where individual and group interests are demonstrably in pure conflict, agreement is not possible, and some rule other than unanimity must normally be introduced to resolve the issue. But where individual and group interests are not clearly defined, where disagreement is based largely on conflicting interpretations concerning the working properties of alternative institutions, discussion and compromise leading to general agreement seem possible.

If observed agreement, or unanimity, provides the only criterion that enables an evaluation of changes in the rules for making political decisions, the question of the starting point becomes important. What position is in being, and what changes are to be considered? Obviously time is wasted if discussion is limited to a hypothetical group of individuals considering the original organization of a political society. The interpretation of the contract theory as applying to such a situation has, I think, plagued much of the critical discussion concerning this theory, and it has obscured the basic validity of the contract approach. A polity exists; it seems best to start from an existing political entity which may best be described in terms of the institutional-constitutional rules for reaching decisions. What is to be sought, therefore, is a criterion for evaluating changes in these existing rules. By saying that agreement or unanimity is the only meaningful criterion in the individualistic context, I of course stand accused of building into the model a defense of the *status quo*. The unique position given to this criterion seems to suggest that whatever exists, is "right," until and unless everyone agrees to make a change, emphasizing, of course, that changes in rules are the sort discussed.

Several points must be made in response to this entirely reasonable interpretation that may be placed on the approach to political process that has been sketched out briefly here. In the first place, it should be noted that no statement at all is made or implied about what is or is not "right," "just," or "correct." The model is based on an explicit disavowal of any personal imputation of moral-ethical values into the system. Secondly, and more important, analysis must start from somewhere, and the existing set of rules and institutions is the only place from which it is possible to start. There is no implication that this position is personally desirable. But if we seek, dispassionately, to evaluate changes, there is no other place from which we may begin. Each and every one of us who looks at the existing political structure might prefer the world to be different from what it is now; but, until and unless general agreement can be reached on making changes, any modification of what exists must involve coercion of some persons by others.

And this means that some choice be made as to which individuals or groups are to be allowed to coerce others, a choice that simply cannot be made without the introduction of external value scales. This need not, of course, inhibit more general discussion. Value scales can be introduced on a personal and necessarily arbitrary, basis, and statements can be made about "socially desired" changes in an existing set of rules. The steps are outside of the model of political process that can be properly called the "individualistic" model. But this is not equivalent to saying that these extraindividualistic models, and whatever theories or hypotheses that they may produce, are somehow "improper." They are simply beyond the pale of this discussion.

Additional clarification may be forthcoming if we return to the poker-game analogy. Assume that play has continued under an agreed-on set of rules for an hour, during which some participants have gained and others lost. A proposal is made to change the rules. The change considered must be from the existing set. Those proposing change may consider the rules wholly unfair and improper, but unless they are prepared to enforce their will on others, they can improve the rules only by securing agreement. Those who accumulated gains under the established rules will not necessarily be averse to reasonable proposals for change. Their positions on a future sequence of plays remain uncertain, and the fact that they have been gaining under one set of rules in no way insures that they will continue to do so. For these reasons, general agreement or consensus becomes possible on changes in rules for future play, as contrasted with the impossibility of agreement on some modified division of gains on a particular play. Clearly, proposals to change the rules of the game through general agreement belong to a different realm of discourse than proposals to change the results that have been generated under an existing set of rules, presumably in accordance with some externally determined value judgment.

Efforts to remain as clear as possible of externally imposed value judgments, to attempt to construct a theory of politics without interjecting interpersonal comparisons, may seem strained and tedious to political scientists. It should again be noted, however, that the approach here taken is derived from theoretical welfare economics. The unanimity criterion is merely the translation into political terms of the familiar Pareto criterion for evaluating changes in policy or in classifying positions.[4] Few economists have extended this criterion to the evaluation of rules or institutions, where it seems considerably more applicable than it does in connection with unique events.[5]

There is an important distinction that is of some significance in understanding the constitutional approach to political rules, one that follows directly from the economist's proclivity to consider human interaction in terms of exchanges. This is the distinction between a zero-sum and a positive-sum game, to use modern, and highly suitable, terminology. In other words, it is necessary to emphasize the difference between situations of pure conflict among individuals and groups and situations that include conflict but also embody mutual possibilities for gain. At the operational level of day-to-day

[4] This criterion states that a position is "optimal" or "efficient" when any change from that position will damage at least one person in the group. There are, of course, an infinite number of positions that may be classified as "optimal." The criterion is useful only for identifying nonoptimal positions. The same criterion may be applied to changes or proposals for change. If a move or change is such that at least one member in the relevant group is made "better off" while no one is made "worse off," the change is "optimal" in Pareto's sense. If a move or change damages at least one person, it is "nonoptimal." If an initial position is "nonoptimal," there must be at least one means of shifting to an "optimal" position in an "optimal" way. The relationship of this construction to the unanimity rule is a direct one once it is admitted that the only way in which an individual can be assured to be made "better off" is as a result of his own observed behavior in making choices.

[5] For a discussion of this extension, see my "The Relevance of Pareto Optimality," *Journal of Conflict Resolution*, VI (December, 1962), 341–54.

politics, where interests of individuals and groups may be sharply identified and delineated, the pure-conflict or zero-sum model can yield useful explanations, as William Riker has demonstrated in his recent work on coalition formation.[6] At the constitutional level of decision, however, where selections must be made among alternative rules, and where individual and group interests are not clearly identified, the situation is not properly described by pure conflict models. Participation in the "great game of politics" must, on balance, be mutually beneficial to all parties, or else revolution would ensue. The game is best conceived as positive-sum. But the game analogy remains relevant. Conflict is not wholly eliminated, and "pure" cooperation (all players on the same side) does not describe the situation.

The ordinary exchange relationship seems to be the appropriate model at this level. Gains can be realized through reaching agreements, and these gains accrue to *all* parties to the relationship, although the distribution of these gains will depend on relative bargaining strengths. Perfect symmetry need not be a property of the result. Unless gains can be secured by *all* parties there is, of course, no possibility that a genuinely voluntary agreement can be attained. Ordinary exchanges, as well as ordinary games, are essentially voluntary because participants are free to withdraw from or to refrain from entering the association. Should the political relationship be viewed, at base, as essentially a voluntary one? That is, of course, the heart of the matter, and the individualistic approach or "theory" of politics comes down squarely on the affirmative side of this question. At the ultimate constitutional level, it seems difficult to talk about political organization unless the structure is assumed to be derived, in some way, from individual consent. If this is not accepted, the basis for any judgment becomes purely personal.

The discussion, to this point, has been devoted largely to presenting a frame of reference within which political process may be examined. The emphasis has been deliberate, for it is the shift in the frame of reference, and not the particulars of analysis, that is the important element in the individualistic approach. It remains, however, to discuss some of the implications that may be drawn from the approach.

It is perhaps evident that the approach is quite consistent with a pragmatic and pluralistic conception of existing political institutions. The test of an institution is whether or not it is predicted to work, not in a unique situation or in a unique period of time, but over a whole sequence of events, over a whole span of time. Workability is not, however, to be measured in terms of accomplishing specifically postulated goals for political action. Such goals are nonexistent in the model. Workability of an institution means the efficacy or efficiency of the institution in accomplishing, for the individual, those purposes or goals, unpredictable at any particular moment of

[6] *The Theory of Political Coalitions* (New Haven: Yale University Press, 1962).

time, that he may desire to achieve from collective action over a sequence of future periods.

Some predictions must be made concerning the adaptability of the institution under varying circumstances. The final estimation of the net efficiency of an institution involves both positive and negative accounts. The political rule or institution must be examined for its positive efficacy in promoting the results that the individual desires to see achieved through political process. But the same rule or institution must be examined also for its negative potentiality for promoting results or outcomes that the individual does not desire. Common sense suggests that different institutions or different rules will be recommended for different types of political decisions.

Tullock and I have analyzed one such institution—the simple majority voting rule—in part for its own intrinsic interest, and, in part, as illustrative of the sort of approach to the various political decision rules that the individualistic conception suggests.[7] Our approach implied that majority voting is not to be prejudged at the outset. It is one possible decision rule among many, and it must stand the test of efficiency when compared to alternative decision rules and institutions. What are the costs of allowing political decisions to be made by majority voting rules? What are the benefits? The point is that these familiar questions should be approached from the vantage point of the individual participant in political process, the citizen-voter-taxpayer-beneficiary. Clearly, if the decision involves choosing among predictable outcomes of a unique, once-and-for-all variety, the single individual could estimate the desirability or undesirability of majority voting rules quite simply by determining whether or not his own opinion is supported by a majority of his fellows. But again, it is not at this level or stage of decision that the rule itself should be evaluated. The individual should be conceived as participating in a "constitutional" decision that ultimately chooses majority rule, or some alternative, on the basis of its predicted effects in producing a whole sequence of outcomes, the particular configurations of which are largely unpredictable.

This "constitutional" choice among political rules and institutions can be subjected to rigorous general analysis that is helpful in indicating the elements that must enter into the individual's final decision. Let us return to the familiar questions concerning the benefits and costs to be expected under the institution of simple majority voting. The individual will recognize that, on a certain number of occasions, he will find himself in the minority, and that, on such occasions, he will be subjected to exploitation by the majority coalition; net costs will be imposed upon him. On the other hand, he will recognize that majority rule is one reasonably simple way of getting decisions made, of getting results accomplished through political process, without excessively high costs of decision. Weighing these two sides of the

---

[7] See *The Calculus of Consent.*

account, he may rationally choose majority rule as "optimal" for certain types of political decisions.

He may, however, reject majority rule for other types of political decisions; he may expect either some less-than-majority rule or some greater-than-majority rule to be more "efficient." His final choice among such rules or institutions will depend on a large number of factors. Prominent among these will be such things as the expected distribution of his own "interest" or "preference" as related to those of his fellows over the expected sequence of issues to be presented, and the expected intensity of this interest on particular sorts of issues. For many aspects of collective organization, where the important consideration becomes the general establishment and acceptance of some rule rather than no rule, the individual may, at the "constitutional" stage, quite rationally choose to delegate final authority to particular individuals in the group. For example, majority rule is obviously inefficient as a means of determining traffic regulations; this task is normally delegated to the bureaucratic apparatus. By contrast, for decisions that can significantly affect human life and property, the individual may choose to accept some "constitutional" constraint that requires greater-than-majority agreement. On such issues, he expects the intensity of his own interest to be such that majority rule will not be acceptable. The familiar constitutional protection to human rights can be "explained" in this way. At a more mundane level, the most familiar example of this sort of thinking is the requirement for variance in municipal zoning laws. Here, in many cases, some greater-than-majority agreement is required to approve proposed changes.

That majority voting is only one among many possibly efficient or inefficient institutions through which political choices are made in a rationally organized democratic structure is recognized in existing political institutions, as the few examples cited above suggest. But this fact seems to be less well established in the literature of political analysis. The divergence here stems, in part, from the "truth judgment" approach to democratic choice that has been previously mentioned. If political decision-structures are viewed, at base, as institutional means of arriving at "correct" decisions, rather than as means of simply reconciling differing individual and group interests, a wholly different conceptual framework of analysis is required. If this essentially nonindividualistic view of politics is accepted, the choice among decision-making institutions must be made on the basis of comparative efficiency in making decisions in terms of some externally established criteria.

Such an approach seems to provide the basis for arguments that decisions had best be left to "experts," to the bureaucrats, who will be able to choose "correctly" with greater efficiency. This is the current antithesis to the individualistic approach to democratic process, and the choice between these fundamentally opposed analytical models can only be made on the acceptance of explicit value judgment. If individual valuations and preferences are to be allowed to count—and this admittedly requires an explicit value judgment—and so long as individuals and groups differ in what they desire to see collectively accomplished, no conceivable computing technique can replace the constitutionally constrained institutions of representative democracy.

One additional implication of the individualistic approach to politics serves to sharpen its contrast with the "truth judgment" model. One of the fundamental "constitutional" decisions that any group must make concerns the appropriate areas of human activity that are to be subject to collective organization. How much collectivization is to be allowed? The answer to this question clearly depends, in the individualistic model, on the rules and institutions that are to prevail in the operation of the collectivized sector. The decisions as to the degree of collectivization and the choice among alternative decision-making institutions are interdependent. It becomes impossible to determine whether or not a particular activity should or should not be collectivized, on efficiency grounds, until the choice among decision-rules is taken into account. This, too, is an obvious but important point that is often overlooked. Collectivization of an activity, say, education, may be highly desirable in a community that is to reach decisions under institutions of majority rule, but highly undesirable in a community that is subjected to dictatorial controls.

The "theory" of democratic political process that has been sketched in this paper suggests a shift in research emphasis. There is required a painstaking and rigorous analysis of existing decision-making institutions in terms of their operation over periods of time and on numbers of issues sufficient to permit meaningful judgments to be made. Both in economics and in politics, attempts must be made to develop theories of institutional structures, and to test the hypotheses derived from these theories against real-world observations. The existing set of institutions surely includes some that are grossly inefficient, as well as others that are highly efficient, even within the limits of an individualistic model. Analysis can highlight these differences and explore the predicted working properties of alternative institutions. This research emphasis follows from an acceptance of the "efficiency" notion that emerges from the individualistic model. Efficiency is not to be defined independently of the choice calculus of the individual citizen as participant in political process.

APPENDIX

The "individualistic" approach to a theory of political process actually represents only one of several strands of recently converging research, which, when taken together promise significant contributions in the social sciences over the next decade. The theory of the firm, which is of course central to orthodox economic analysis, is only now being re-examined under the assumption that a business firm is not to be studied as a single person, but as an organization within which the several persons involved variously interact one with another. Bureaucratic structures, within or without government, are similarly under theoretical reappraisal, and the conflicts between individual and organizational goals and the impact of these conflicts on behavior and performance have come to be recognized as important elements of scientific investigation. And there are many other similar examples.

Contributions from organization theory, information theory, the theory of teams, statistical decision theory, game theory, learning theory, theoretical welfare economics, pure theory of government finance, and others point toward a fundamental revision of existing orthodoxy, and an emerging consensus on what may be called a general theory of social structures, which will surely include political organization as only one among an array of forms. These developments should help to break down the barriers among the disciplinary specializations in the social sciences, barriers which have been, at best, arbitrarily erected and maintained.

THREE

JAMES G. MARCH

University of California, Irvine

*The Power of Power**

1.0 INTRODUCTION

Power is a major explanatory concept in the study of social choice. It is used in studies of relations among nations, of community decision making, of business behavior, and of small-group discussion. Partly because it conveys simultaneously overtones of the cynicism of *Realpolitik,* the glories of classical mechanics, the realism of elite sociology, and the comforts of anthropocentric theology, *power* provides a prime focus for disputation and exhortation in several social sciences.

Within this galaxy of nuances, I propose to consider a narrowly technical question: To what extent is one specific concept of power useful in the empirical analysis of mechanisms for social choice? The narrowness of the question is threefold. First, only theories that focus on mechanisms of choice are considered. Second, only considerations of utility for the development or testing of empirically verifiable theories are allowed. Third,

[This paper received the American Political Science Association Pi Sigma Alpha Award for the best paper presented at the Association's annual meetings in 1963—Ed.]

* The paper has profited considerably from the comments of John C. Harsanyi, Herbert Kaufman, Norton E. Long, Duncan MacRae, Jr., Dale T. Mortensen, and Raymond E. Wolfinger, and by a pre-publication reading of Robert A. Dahl's forthcoming article, "The Power Analysis Approach to the Study of Politics," in the *International Encyclopedia of the Social Sciences.*

only one concept of power—or one class of concepts—is treated. The question is technical in the sense that it has primary relevance for the drudgery of constructing a predictive theory; the immediate implications for general theories of society, for the layman confronted with his own complex environment, or for the casual student, are probably meager. They certainly are not developed here.

By a mechanism for social choice, I mean nothing more mysterious than a committee, jury, legislature, commission, bureaucracy, court, market, firm, family, gang, mob, and various combinations of these into economic, political, and social systems. Despite their great variety, each of these institutions can be interpreted as a mechanism for amalgamating the behavior (preferences, actions, decisions) of subunits into the behavior of the larger institution; thus, each acts as a mechanism for social choice. The considerations involved in evaluating the usefulness of power as a concept are the same for all of the mechanisms cited above, although it is patently not necessarily true that the conclusions need be the same.

By an empirically verifiable theory, I mean a theory covered by the standard dicta about prediction and confirmation. We will ask under what circumstances the use of *power* contributes to the predictive power of the theory.

The specific concept of power I have in mind is the concept used in theories having the following general assumptions:

1. The choice mechanism involves certain basic components (individuals, groups, roles, behaviors, labels, etc.).
2. Some amount of power is associated with each of these components.
3. The responsiveness (as measured by some direct empirical observation) of the mechanism to each individual component is monotone increasing with the power associated with the individual component.

There are a number of variations on this general theme, each with idiosyncratic problems; but within a well-defined (and relatively large) class of uses of the concept of power, power plays the same basic role. It is a major intervening variable between an initial condition, defined largely in terms of the individual components of the system, and a terminal state, defined largely in terms of the system as a whole.

In order to explore the power of power in empirical theories of social choice, I propose to do two things: First, I wish to identify three different variations in this basic approach to power as an intervening variable to suggest the kinds of uses of *power* with which we will be concerned. Second, I wish to examine six different classes of models of social choice that are generally consistent with what at least one substantial group of students means by *social power*. In this examination, I will ask what empirical and technical problems there are in the use of the concept of power and in the use of alternative concepts, and under what circumstances the concept of power does, or can, contribute to the effective prediction of social choice.

2.0 THREE APPROACHES TO
THE STUDY OF POWER

2.1 The experimental study

The great variety of types of studies of power in the experimental literature is clear from a perusal of recent compendia and review articles.[1] Since many of these studies are only marginally relevant to the concerns of this paper, I will assume general awareness of the experimental literature rather than attempt to review it. This brief introduction is intended simply to provide a relatively coherent characterization of a class of approaches to the study of power. Although these approaches are predominantly used in experimental studies, the experimental setting is neither a necessary nor a sufficient condition for the approaches; the label "experimental studies" is simply shorthand for the general approach.

Conceptual basis. The experimental studies of power are generally Newtonian. Many of them are directly indebted to Lewin, who defined the power of *b* over *a* "as the quotient of the maximum force which *b* can induce on *a,* and the maximum resistance which *a* can offer."[2] In general, the experimental studies assume that the greater the power of the individual, the greater the changes induced (with given resistance) and the more successful the resistance to changes (with given pressure to change).

The experimental studies tend to be reductionist. Although they are ultimately (and sometimes immediately) interested in the power of one individual over another, they usually seek to reduce that relationship to more basic components. Thus, we distinguish between the power of behavior and the power of roles, and characterize specific individuals as a combination of behavior and roles.[3] Or, we distinguish factors affecting the agent of influence, the methods of influence, and the agent subjected to influence.[4]

The experimental studies of interest here are generally synthetic. They attempt to predict the result of the interaction of known (experimentally manipulated) forces rather than to determine the forces by analysis of known (or hypothetical) results. The problem is generally not to determine the power distribution, but to test the consequences of various power distributions.

[1] See Dorwin Cartwright, ed., *Studies in Social Power* (Ann Arbor: University of Michigan Press, 1959); Dorwin Cartwright and A. F. Zander, eds., *Group Dynamics* (New York: Harper & Row, Publishers, 1959); and Dorwin Cartwright, "Influence, Leadership, Control," in *Handbook of Organizations,* ed. J. G. March (Chicago: Rand McNally & Co., 1965).

[2] Kurt Lewin, *Field Theory in Social Science* (New York: Harper & Row, Publishers, 1951), p. 336.

[3] See J. G. March, "Measurement Concepts in the Theory of Influence," *Journal of Politics,* XIX (1957), 202–26.

[4] See Cartwright, "Influence, Leadership, Control."

Procedures. The procedures used in this class of experimental studies are the classic ones. We determine power by some a priori measure or experimental manipulation, use a relatively simple force model to generate hypotheses concerning differences in outcomes from different treatments, and compare the observed outcomes with the predicted outcomes.

One of the better known variations on the basic Lewinian model is the one by French as further developed by Harary.[5] In this model, we predict shifts in opinion as a result of communication among subjects characterized by initial positions. Power exerted in a given direction is a function of the distribution of underlying power and the distances between the initial positions. In the two-person version of the model, change in opinion is inversely proportional to power. If we view an *n*-person group as being connected by a communication structure defining who can (or does) talk to whom, the model predicts the time series of opinion changes and the equilibrium opinions for various power distributions and communication structures. Theorems for the equal-power case are presented by French and Harary. Few theorems have been adduced for the unequal-power case in general, but the model can easily be used to generate specific predictions in specific cases.

Although few other models approach the specificity of the graph-theory version, the inverse relation between opinion- or behavior-change and power is normally used to derive hypotheses about differences among treatments.

Results. There are several studies of social power that are substantially irrelevant for the present discussion. Studies of the consequences of apparent power for nontask or non-opinion behavior are potentially relevant, but they have rarely been interpreted in a way that fits this framework. For example, the responses to power are classified nominally, rather than along a continuum. Similarly, many of the studies of factors in differential influence (e.g., content of the communication) are only marginally relevant here.

For present purposes, two general results are particularly germane:

(1) It is possible to vary power of a specific subject systematically and (within limits) arbitrarily in an experimental setting. This can be done by manipulating some elements of his reputation[6] or by manipulating some elements of his power experience.[7] This apparently innocuous—and cer-

---

[5] See J. R. P. French, Jr., "A Formal Theory of Social Power," *Psychological Review,* LXIII (1956), 181–94; and Cartwright, *Studies in Social Power.*

[6] See C. I. Hovland, I. L. Janis, and H. H. Kelley, *Communication and Persuasion* (New Haven: Yale University Press, 1953).

[7] See B. Mausner, "The Effect of Prior Reinforcement on the Interaction of Observer Pairs," *Journal of Abnormal and Social Psychology,* XLIX (1954), 65–68, and "The Effect of One Partner's Success or Failure in a Relevant Task on the Interaction of Observer Pairs," *Journal of Abnormal and Social Psychology,* XLIX (1954), 577–60.

tainly minimal—result is in fact not so unimportant. It permits us to reject certain kinds of social-choice models for certain kinds of situations.

(2) The effectiveness of a priori power (i.e., manipulated, or a priori measured power) in producing behavior change is highly variable. Although there are indications that some kinds of leadership behavior are exhibited by some people in several different groups,[8] most studies indicate that the effectiveness of specific individuals, specific social positions, and specific behaviors in producing behavior change varies with respect to the content and relevancy of subject matter,[9] group identifications,[10] and power base.[11] In fact, much of the literature is devoted to identifying these factors.

2.2 The community study

A second major approach to the study of power can be called *the community power approach;* it is typical of, but not limited to, community studies.[12] This paper is limited to the basic problems of power and consequently does not do justice to the variety of substantive concerns represented in the research. As in the case of the experimental literature, it also exaggerates the conceptual homogeneity of the studies; I think, though, that there is general homogeneity with respect to the questions of interest here.

Conceptual basis. The conceptual definition of power implicit (and often explicit) in the community studies is clearly Newtonian. The first two "laws" of social choice form a simple definition:

1. Social choice will be a predictable extension of past choices unless power is exerted on the choice.
2. When power is exerted, the modification of the choice will be proportional to the power.

The laws may lack some of the operational precision of Newton; in fact, it is not clear that they are any more Newton than Aristotle. But the community power studies generally assume that the decisions made by the community are a function of the power exerted on the community by various power holders. They assume some kind of "power field" in which individual powers are summed to produce the final outcome.

The community studies are analytic in the sense that they attempt to infer the power of individuals within the community by observing (either

[8] See E. F. Borgatta, A. S. Couch, and R. F. Bales, "Some Findings Relevant to the Great Man Theory of Leadership," *American Sociological Review,* XIX (1954), 755–59.

[9] J. G. March, "Influence Measurement in Experimental and Semi-Experimental Groups," *Sociometry,* XIX (1956), 260–71.

[10] Cartwright, *Studies in Social Power.*

[11] Cartwright, *Studies in Social Power.*

[12] For reviews of the literature, see P. H. Rossi, "Community Decision Making," *Administrative Science Quarterly,* I (1957), 415–43; and L. J. R. Herson, "In the Footsteps of Community Power," *American Political Science Review,* LV (1961), 817–30.

directly or indirectly) their net effects on community choice. That is, they assume that a decision is some function of individual powers and the individual preferences. Hence, they observe the decision outcome and the preferences, and estimate the powers.

The community studies are personal in the sense that power is associated with specific individuals. The estimation procedures are designed to determine the power of an individual. This power, in turn, is viewed as some function of the resources (economic, social, etc.), position (office, role, etc.), and skill (choice of behavior, choice of allies, etc.); but the study and the analysis assume that it is meaningful to aggregate resource power, position power, and skill power into a single variable associated with the individual.

Procedures. The controversy over the procedures used in community studies is well-known.[13] Since that controversy forms part of the background to the more general discussion below, I will simply lay the descriptive groundwork here. The procedure most generally used involves some variation of asking individuals within the community to assess the relative power of other individuals in the community. Essentially the panel is given the following task: On the basis of past experience (both your own and that of other people with whom you have communicated), estimate the power of the following individuals.[14] In some cases the domain of power is specified only broadly (e.g., political decisions); in some cases it is specified relatively narrowly (e.g., urban renewal decisions).

A second procedure involves the direct observation of decision outcomes and prior preferences over a series of decisions.[15] Essentially, we define a model relating power to decisions, draw a sample of observations, and estimate the power of individuals on the basis of that model and those observations.

It seems rather clear that neither the direct nor the indirect method of estimation is necessarily better. As we will note below, there are many "reasonable" models of power; and the estimation problems are somewhat different for the different models.

Results. At a general level, the results of the community studies can

[13] See W. V. D'Antonio and H. J. Ehrlich, *Power and Democracy in America* (South Bend, Ind.: Notre Dame University Press, 1961); W. V. D'Antonio and E. C. Erickson, "The Reputational Technique as a Measure of Community Power: An Evaluation Based on Comparative and Longitudinal Studies," *American Sociological Review*, XXVII (1962), 362–76; N. W. Polsby, "Three Problems in the Analysis of Community Power," *American Sociological Review*, XXIV (1959), 796–803; N. W. Polsby, "Community Power: Some Reflections on the Recent Literature," *American Sociological Review*, XXVII (1962), 838–41; and R. E. Wolfinger, "Reputation and Reality in the Study of 'Community Power,'" *American Sociological Review*, XXV (1960), 636–44.

[14] See F. Hunter, *Community Power Structures* (Chapel Hill: University of North Carolina Press, 1953).

[15] See R. A. Dahl, *Who Governs?* (New Haven: Yale University Press, 1961).

be described in terms of three broad types of interests. First, we ask how power is distributed in the community. Second, we ask what relation exists between power and the possession of certain other socioeconomic attributes. Third, we ask how power is exerted.

With respect to the distribution of power, most studies indicate that most people in most communities are essentially powerless. They neither participate in the making of decisions directly nor accumulate reputations for power. Whatever latent control they may have, it is rarely exercised. As a result, such control cannot be demonstrated by the power-measurement procedures of the community studies. Beyond the simple statement that only a minority of the population appears to exercise power, the studies are not really designed to elaborate the description of the power distribution. Some general statements of comparative variances can be made, but nothing approximating a systematic measure of power variance has been reported.

With respect to the relation between power and other individual characteristics, rather sharp differences among communities have been observed. Two results are conspicuous. First, in every study reported, the business and economic elite is overrepresented (in terms of chance expectations) among the high power holders. By any of these measures, the economic notable is more powerful in the community than the average man. Second, the main influences on the extent to which noneconomic characteristics are found to be important seem to be the procedures used in the investigation and the academic license of the investigator.[16] On the whole, studies using the general reputational technique seem to show business-economic characteristics[17] as more important than do studies using the direct-observation technique or a more narrowly defined reputation.[18] And studies by sociologists usually show business-economic characteristics as more important than do studies by political scientists. The two factors are hopelessly cross-contaminated, of course; and there are exceptions. If we assume that the correlation between results and technique (or discipline) is spurious, it may be possible to argue that the results are consistent with the hypothesis that power in somewhat older communities (e.g., English City, New Haven) is less linked to economic factors than is power in somewhat newer communities (e.g., Regional City, Pacific City).

With respect to the exercise of power, the studies have focused on specialization, activation, and unity of power holders. Most studies have identified significant specialization in power: Different individuals are powerful with respect to different things. But most studies also have shown

16 See N. W. Polsby, "The Sociology of Community Power: A Reassessment," *Social Forces*, XXXVII (1959), 232–36; and P. Bachrach and M. S. Baratz, "Two Faces of Power," *American Political Science Review*, LVI (1962), 947–52.
17 See, for example, Hunter, *Community Power Structures*.
18 See, for example, Dahl, *Who Governs?*

"general leaders": Some individuals have significant power in several areas. Some studies have reported a significant problem associated with power activation: the more powerful members of the community are not necessarily activated to use their power, while less powerful members may be hyperactivated. The activation factor may be long-run[19] or short-run.[20] Although few systematic observations have been used to explore unity among the powerful, there has been some controversy on the extent to which the group of more powerful individuals represents a cohesive group with respect to community decisions. Some studies indicate a network of associations, consultations, and agreements among the more powerful; other studies indicate rather extensive disagreement among the more powerful.[21]

2.3 The institutional study

The third alternative approach to the study of power is in one sense the most common of all. It is the analysis of the structure of institutions to determine the power structure within them. Such studies are the basis of much of descriptive political science. Systematic attempts to derive quantitative indices of power from an analysis of institutional structure are limited, however. The approach will be characterized here in terms of the game-theory version, but other alternative a priori institutional interpretations of power would fall in the same class.[22]

The possibility of using the Shapley value for an n-person game as the basis for a power index has intrigued a number of students of bargaining and social-decision systems.[23] The present discussion will assume a general knowledge of game theory, the Shapley value,[24] and the original Shapley and Shubik article.[25]

[19] See Dahl, *Who Governs?*

[20] See R. C. Hanson, "Predicting a Community Decision: A Test of the Miller-Form Theory," *American Sociological Review,* XXIV (1959), 662–71.

[21] See W. H. Form and W. V. D'Antonio, "Integration and Cleavage among Community Influentials in Two Border Cities," *American Sociological Review,* XXIV (1959), 804–14; and H. Scoble, "Leadership Hierarchies and Political Issues in a New England Town," in *Community Political Systems,* ed. Morris Janowitz (New York: Free Press of Glencoe, Inc., 1961).

[22] See, for example, Karl Marx, *Capital* (New York, 1906).

[23] Dahl, *Who Governs?* and H. A. Simon, *Models of Man* (New York: John Wiley & Sons, Inc., 1957), both of whom are conceptually much closer to the other approaches outlined here, seem to have been supportive. W. H. Riker, "A Test of the Adequacy of the Power Index," *Behavioral Science,* IV (1959), 276–90, applies the value in an empirical study; and J. C. Harsanyi, "Measurement of Social Power, Opportunity Costs, and the Theory of Two-Person Bargaining Games," *Behavioral Science,* VII (1962), 67–80, extends the value.

[24] L. S. Shapley, "A Value for n-Person Games," in *Contributions to the Theory of Games,* eds. H. W. Huhn and A. W. Tucker (Princeton: Princeton University Press, 1953), II.

[25] L. S. Shapley and M. Shubik, "A Method for Evaluating the Distribution of Power in a Committee System," *American Political Science Review,* XLVIII (1954), 787–92.

Conceptual basis. The Shapley value is Neumannian. We assume the general von Neumann concept of a game: There are *n* players, each with a well-defined set of alternative strategies. Given the choice of strategies by the player (including the mutual choice of coalitions), there is a well-defined set of rules for determining the outcome of the game. The outcomes are evaluated by the individual players in terms of the individual orderings of preference. The Shapley value for the game to an individual player (or coalition of players) has several alternative intuitive explanations. It can be viewed as how much a rational person would be willing to pay in order to occupy a particular position in the game rather than some other position. It can be viewed as the expected marginal contribution of a particular position to a coalition if all coalitions are considered equally likely and the order in which positions are added to the coalition is random. It can be viewed as how much a rational player would expect to receive from a second rational player in return for his always selecting the strategy dictated by the second player. Or, it can be viewed simply as a computational scheme with certain desirable properties of uniqueness.

The Shapley value is impersonal. It is associated not with a specific player but rather with a specific position in the game. It is not conceived to measure the power of President Kennedy or President Eisenhower; it is conceived to measure the power of the Presidency.

The value is analytic in the sense that it is derived from the rules of the game (e.g., the legislative scheme) rather than vice versa. The value is a priori in the sense that it does not depend on empirical observations and has no necessary empirical implications.

How do we move from such a conception of value to a conception of power? One way is to restrict ourselves to a parsimonious definition: "When we use the word *power* in the rest of this paper, it shall mean only the numerical representation of rewards accruing to coalitions as evaluated by the members of these coalitions."[26] Although such a procedure is defensible, it will not help us significantly in the present discussion. We need to relate the Shapley-Shubik measure to the Newtonian approaches previously described. In the standard Newtonian versions of power, power is that which induces a modification of choice by the system. Quite commonly, we measure the power by the extent to which the individual is able to induce the system to provide resources of value to him. We are aware that power, in this sense, is a function of many variables; we suspect that informal alliances and allegiances influence behavior; and we commonly allege that power is dependent on information and intelligence as well as formal position.

Suppose that we want to assess the contribution to power of formal position alone. One way to do so would be an empirical study in which we

[26] R. D. Luce and A. A. Rogow, "A Game Theoretic Analysis of Congressional Power Distributions for a Stable Two-Party System," *Behavioral Science,* I (1956), 85.

would consider simultaneously all of the various contributing factors, apply some variant of a multiple regression technique, and determine the appropriate coefficients for the position variables. A second way would be an experimental study in which nonposition factors are systematically randomized. A third way would be the one taken by Shapley and Shubik. We can imagine a game involving position variables only (e.g., the formal legislative scheme), and we can assume rationality on the part of the participants and ask for the value of each position under that assumption. Since this value is a direct measure of the resources the individual can obtain from the system by virtue of his position in the game alone, it is a reasonable measure of the power of that position. Alternatively, we can view the resources themselves as power.[27]

Procedures. There are two main ways in which we can use the Shapley-Shubik index in an empirical study: (1) We can construct some sort of empirical index of power, make some assumptions about the relation between the empirical and a priori measures, and test the consistency of the empirical results with the a priori measures. Thus, we might assume that the empirical measure consists of the a priori measure plus an error term representing various other (nonposition) factors. If we can make some assumptions about the nature of the "error," we can test the consistency. Or, (2), we can deduce some additional propositions from the model underlying the index and test those propositions.

The first of these alternatives was suggested by Shapley and Shubik and considered by Riker. But neither they nor others have seen a way around the major obstacles in the way. The second alternative was the basis for a series of papers by Luce, Rogow, and Riker.[28]

Results. The main results in the application of the Shapley value have had only casual testing. Luce and Rogow have used the basic Shapley-Shubik approach in conjunction with Luce's conception of $\emptyset$-stability to generate some power distributions consistent with a stable two-party system. In this approach, one first assumes a two-party legislature and a President belonging to one of the two parties. Within each party, there is a subset that always votes with the party, a subset that is willing to defect to the other party, and a subset that is willing to form a coalition with a defecting subset from the other party. The President may be constrained always to vote with his party or to defect only to the coalition of defectors. Alternatively, he may be completely free to defect. This legislature operates under some voting rules which define (along with the size of parties, the

[27] See R. D. Luce, "Further Comments on Power Distributions for a Stable Two-Party Congress," Paper read at American Political Science Association meetings (1956); and Riker, "A Test of the Adequacy of the Power Index."

[28] Luce and Rogow, "A Game Theoretic Analysis"; Luce, "Further Comments on Power Distributions"; and Riker, "A Test of the Adequacy of the Power Index."

permissible defections, and the size of defecting subsets) a set of coalitions that are able to pass a bill. The analysis produces a series of observations on the stability and other properties of power distributions found under various combinations of restrictions on the President and the size of the party subsets. These detailed results lead then to more general statements of the form: "The richer the defection possibilities . . . the greater the localization of power."[29] Although some of the results obtained seem intuitively sensible, only a footnoted bit of data has been adduced in support of them. In fact, most of the propositions are stated in a form that would require an empirical measure of power—and that would drive us back to the difficulty previously observed.

Riker has applied the basic Shapley-Shubik measure to the French Assembly to derive changes in power indices for the various parties in the French Assembly during the period 1953–54, as thirty-four migrations from one party to another produced sixty-one individual changes in affiliation.[30] On the assumption that party power is equally distributed among individual members, Riker tested the proposition that shifts in party affiliation tended to result in increases in individual power. The data did not support the hypothesis. In subsequent work, Riker has almost entirely abandoned the Shapley-Shubik approach.[31]

3.0 SIX MODELS OF SOCIAL CHOICE AND THE CONCEPT OF POWER

The three general approaches described above illustrate the range of possible uses of the concept of power, and include most of the recent efforts to use the concept in empirical research or in empirically oriented theory. I wish to use these three examples as a basis for exploring the utility of the concept of power in the analysis of systems for social choice. The utility depends first, on the true characteristics of the system under investigation. The concept of power must be embedded in a model and the validity of the model is a prerequisite to the utility of the concept. Second, the utility depends on the technical problems of observation, estimation, and validation in using the concept in an empirically reasonable model.

I shall now consider six types of models of social choice, evaluate their consistency with available data, and consider the problems of the concept of power associated with them. By a *model* I mean a set of statements about the way in which individual choices (or behavior) are transformed into social choices, and a procedure for using those statements to derive some empirically meaningful predictions. The six types of models are:

[29] Luce, "Further Comments on Power Distributions," p. 10.
[30] Riker, "A Test of the Adequacy of the Power Index."
[31] W. H. Riker, *The Theory of Political Coalitions* (New Haven: Yale University Press, 1962).

1. Chance models, in which we assume that choice is a chance event, quite independent of power.
2. Basic force models, in which we assume that the components of the system exert all their power on the system with choice being a direct resultant of those powers.
3. Force activation models, in which we assume that not all the power of every component is exerted at all times.
4. Force-conditioning models, in which we assume that the power of the components is modified as a result of the outcome of past choices.
5. Force depletion models, in which we assume that the power of the components is modified as a result of the exertion of power on past choices.
6. Process models, in which we assume that choice is substantially independent of power but not a chance event.

The list is reasonably complete insofar as we are interested in empirically oriented models of social choice. The approaches to the study of social power previously discussed and a fair number of other theories of social choice can be fitted into the framework.

3.1 Chance models

Let us assume that there are no attributes of human beings affecting the output of a social-choice mechanism. Further, let us assume that the only factors influencing the output are chance factors, constrained perhaps by some initial conditions. There are a rather large number of such models, but it will be enough here to describe three in skeleton form.

The unconstrained model. We assume a set of choice alternatives given to the system. These might be all possible bargaining agreements in bilateral bargaining, all possible appropriations in a legislative scheme, or all experimentally defined alternatives in an experimental setting. Together with this set of alternatives, we have a probability function. Perhaps the simplest form of the function would be one that made the alternatives discrete, finite, and equally probable; but we can allow any form of function so long as the probabilities do not depend on the behavior, attitudes, or initial position of the individual components in the system.

The equal-power model. We assume a set of initial positions for the components of the system and some well-defined procedures for defining a social choice consistent with the assumption of equal power. For example, the initial positions might be arranged on some simple continuum. We might observe the initial positions with respect to wage rates in collective bargaining, with respect to legislative appropriations for space exploration, or with respect to the number of peas in a jar in an experimental group. A simple arithmetic mean of such positions is a social choice consistent with the assumption of equal power. In this chance model, we assume that the social choice is the equal-power choice plus some error term. In the simplest case, we assume that the error around the equal-power choice is random and normally distributed with mean zero and a variance that is some function of the variance of initial positions.

The encounter model. We assume only two possible choice outcomes: We can win or lose; the bill can pass or fail; we will take the left or right branch in the maze. At each encounter (social choice) there are two opposing teams. The probability of choosing a given alternative if the teams have an equal number of members is 0.5. If the teams are unequal in size, we have three broad alternatives:

1. We can make the probability of choosing the first alternative a continuous monotone increasing function of the disparity between the sizes of the two teams.
2. We can assume that the larger teams always wins.
3. We can assume that the probability is 0.5 regardless of the relative sizes of the teams, thus making the model a special case of the unconstrained model.

What are the implications of such models? Consider the encounter model. Suppose we imagine that each power encounter occurs between just two people chosen at random from the total population of the choice system. Further, assume that at each encounter we will decide who prevails by flipping a coin.[32] If the total number of encounters per person is relatively small and the total number of persons relatively large, such a process will yield a few people who are successful in their encounters virtually all the time, others who are successful most of the time, and so on. In a community of 4000 adults and about a dozen encounters per adult, we would expect about 12 or 13 adults to have been unsuccessful no more than once. Similarly, if we assume that all encounters are between teams and that assignment to teams is random, the other encounter models above will yield identical results. A model of this general class has been used by Deutsch and Madow to generate a distribution of managerial performance and reputations.[33]

Similar kinds of results can be obtained from the unconstrained-chance model. If we assume that social choice is equi-probable among the alternatives and that individual initial positions are equi-probable among the alternatives, the only difference is that the number of alternatives is no longer

[32] See H. White, "Uses of Mathematics in Sociology," in *Mathematics and the Social Sciences,* ed. J. C. Charlesworth (Philadelphia: American Academy of Political and Social Science, 1963).

[33] K. W. Deutsch and W. G. Madow, "A Note on the Appearance of Wisdom in Large Organizations," *Behavioral Science,* VI (1961), 72–78.

necessarily two. In general, there will be more than two alternatives; as a result the probability of success will be less than 0.5 on every trial and the probability of a long-run record of spectacular success correspondingly less. For example, if we assume a dozen trials with ten alternatives, the probability of failing no more than once drops to about 10^{-10} (as compared with about .0032 in the two alternative cases).

Finally, generally similar results are obtained from the equal-power model. If we assume that the initial position is normally distributed with mean, M, and variance, V, and that the error is normally distributed around M with a variance that is some function of V, we obtain what amounts to variations in the continuous version of the discrete models. If we set the error variance equal to V, the relationship is obvious. Our measures of success now become not the number (or proportion) of successes but rather the mean deviation of social choices from individual positions; and we generate from the model a distribution of such distances for a given number of trials.[34]

All of the chance models generate power distributions. They are spurious distributions in the sense that power, as we usually mean it, had nothing to do with what happened. But we can still apply our measures of power to the systems involved. After observing such a system, one can make statements about the distribution of power in the system and describe how power was exercised. Despite these facts, I think that most students of power would agree that if a specific social-choice system is in fact a chance mechanism, the concept of power is not a valuable concept for that system.

To what extent is it possible to reject the chance models in studies of social choice? Although there are some serious problems in answering that question, I think we would probably reject a pure-chance model as a reasonable model. I say this with some trepidation because studies of power have generally not considered such alternative models, and many features of many studies are certainly consistent with a chance interpretation. The answer depends on an evaluation of four properties of the chance models that are potentially inconsistent with data either from field studies or from the laboratory.

First, we ask whether power is stable over time. With most of the chance models, knowing who won in the past or who had a reputation for winning in the past would not help us to predict who would win in the future. Hence, if we can predict the outcome of future social choices by weighting current positions with weights derived from past observations or from a priori considerations, we will have some justification for rejecting the chance model. Some efforts have been made in this direction, but with mixed results.[35] Even conceding the clarity of the tests and the purity of the procedures and assuming that the results were all in the predicted direction,

[34] See D. MacRae, Jr., and H. D. Price, "Scale Positions and 'Power' in the Senate," *Behavioral Science*, IV (1959), 212–18.

[35] See, for example, Hanson, "Predicting a Community Decision."

the argument for the various power models against a chance model would be meager. The "powerful" would win about half the time even under the chance hypothesis.

Second, we ask whether power is stable over subject matter. Under the chance models, persons who win in one subject-matter area would be no more likely to win in another area than would people who lost in the first area. Thus, if we find a greater-than-chance overlap from one area to another, we would be inclined to reject the chance model. The evidence on this point is conflicting. As was noted earlier, some studies suggest considerable specialization of power, while others do not. On balance, I find it difficult to reject the chance model on the basis of these results; although it is clear that there are a number of alternative explanations for the lack of stability, nonchance explanations are generally preferred by persons who have observed subject-matter instability.[36]

Third, we ask whether power is correlated with other personal attributes. Under the chance model, power is independent of other attributes. Although it might occasionally be correlated with a specific set of attributes by chance, a consistent correlation would cast doubt on the chance hypothesis. It would have to be saved by some assumption about the inadequacy (that is, irrelevance) of the power measure or by assuming that the covariation results from an effect of power on the correlated attribute. Without any exception of which I am aware, the studies do show a greater-than-chance relation between power and such personal attributes as economic status, political office, and ethnic group. We cannot account under the simple chance model for the consistent underrepresentation of the poor, the unelected, and the Negro.

And fourth, we ask whether power is *susceptible to experimental manipulation*. If the chance model were correct, we could not systematically produce variations in who wins by manipulating power. Here the experimental evidence is fairly clear. It is possible to manipulate the results of choice mechanisms by manipulating personal attributes or personal reputations. Although we may still want to argue that the motivational or institutional setting of real-world choice systems is conspicuously different from the standard experimental situation, we cannot sustain a strictly chance interpretation of the experimental results.

Chance models are extremely naïve; they are the weakest test we can imagine. Yet we have had some difficulty in rejecting them, and in some situations it is not clear that we can reject them. Possibly much of what happens in the world is by chance. If so, it will be a simple world to deal with. Possibly, however, our difficulty is not with the amount of order in the world, but with the concept of power. Before we can render any kind of judgment on that issue, we need to consider some models that might be considered more reasonable by people working in the field.

[36] See, for example, N. W. Polsby, "How to Study Community Power: The Pluralist Alternative," *Journal of Politics,* XXII (1960), 474–84.

3.2 Basic force models

Suppose we assume that power is real and controlling, and start with a set of models that are closely linked with classical mechanics although the detailed form is somewhat different from mechanics. In purest form, the simple force models can be represented in terms of functions that make the resultant social choice a weighted average of the individual initial positions—the weights being the power attached to the various individuals. Let us identify three variations on this theme:

The continuous case. Let C_j be the outcome (social choice) on the jth issue and A_{ij} be the initial position on the jth issue of the ith individual power source. C_j and the A_{ij} may be vectors, but they have the same dimensions. Let m_{ij}° be the total power resources available to the ith component at the jth issue, and let m_{ij} be the normalized form of this. Thus:

$$m_{ij} = m_{ij}^{\circ} / \sum_{i=1}^{n} m_{ij}^{\circ},$$

where n is the number of components.

The basic force model, in which we assume that m_{ij}° is a constant over all j, is elegant in its simplicity:

$$C_j = \sum_{i=1}^{n} m_i A_{ij}.$$

Given a set of power indices and initial positions, we can predict the outcomes. Given a set of outcomes and the associated initial positions, we can determine the power indices.

The probabilistic binary case. Suppose C_j and A_{ij} can assume only two values (yes-no, pro-con, pass-fail, up-down, etc.). Associate the nominal values 1 and -1 with the two alternatives. Let P_j be the probability that $C_j = 1$. Then the basic force model assumes the form

$$P_j = \frac{1 + \sum_{i=1}^{n} m_i A_{ij}}{2}.$$

Alternatively, we can define any function that maps $(-1, 1)$ onto $(0, 1)$, is monotone increasing, and is symmetric around the point $(0, 0.5)$. Most data suggest, in fact, that the function is not linear.[37]

Given the function, a set of power indices, and the initial positions, we can predict the outcomes subject to some chance error.

[37] F. M. Tonge, "Models of Majority Influence in Unanimous Group Decision," Unpublished (1963).

Given the function, a set of outcomes, and the associated initial positions, we can determine the power indices subject to some errors in estimation.

The nearly determinate binary case. In this special form of the binary case, we assume that the more powerful team carries the day unequivocally. Thus

$$P_j = \left\{ \begin{matrix} 1 \\ .5 \\ 0 \end{matrix} \right\} \text{ if } \sum_{i=1}^{n} m_i A_{ij} \left\{ \begin{matrix} > \\ = \\ < \end{matrix} \right\} 0.$$

As before, we can use the model to predict outcomes given the power and initial positions, or to estimate power given outcomes and initial positions. In the latter case, we would normally have a family of solutions rather than a single solution.

The only serious problem with the use of these models lies in potential difficulties in estimation. But it is clear that the estimation problems are relatively minor unless the required observations are difficult to obtain. Consider the continuous case. Since we know that

$$m_k = \frac{C_j - \sum_{i \neq k} m_i A_{ij}}{A_{kj}} \qquad i = 1, \dots, n$$

we need only $n-1$ distinct observations to determine the power (m_k) weights in a system having n distinct power sources. If the system involves only two individuals, we require only one observation to determine the weights. We get similar results in the case of the nearly determinate binary case, although we deal in inequalities. If we ignore the possibility of a tie between the two sides, we know that

$$m_k < C_j \sum_{i \neq k} m_i A_{ij} \qquad i = 1, \dots, \text{n.}$$

Thus, given a set of observations we can define a family of values for the m_i that are consistent with the observations.

In the probabilistic case, the observations are the basis for estimating a set of weights that control the results (outcomes) only up to a probability value. If we have s observations, we know that

$$m_k = \frac{1 - 2 \sum_{j=1}^{s} P_j - \sum_{i \neq k} \sum_{j=1}^{s} m_i A_{ij}}{\sum_{j=1}^{s} A_{kj}} \qquad i = 1, \dots, \text{n.}$$

However, we do not know $\sum_{j=1}^{s} P_j$, but have to estimate it from $\sum_{j=1}^{s} C_j$. As a result, our estimate of m_k is subject to sampling variation.

None of these estimation problems are severe. In fact, the first two models are determinate and trivial; the third involves the binomial distribution but is not overly complicated.

The force models, therefore, are reasonably well-defined and pose no great technical problems, and the estimation procedures are straightforward. The observations required are no more than the observations required by any model that assumes some sort of power. What are the implications of the models? First, unless combined with a set of constraints (such as the power-structure constraints of the French and Harary formulation), the models say nothing about the distribution of power in a choice system. Thus, there is no way to test their apparent plausibility by comparing actual power distributions with derived distributions.

Second, in all of the models, the distance between the initial position of the individual and the social choice (or expected social choice) is inversely proportional to the power when we deal with just two individuals. As we noted earlier, this is also a property of French's model. With more than two individuals, the relation between distance and power becomes more complex, depending on the direction and magnitude of the various forces applied to the system. Since the models are directly based on the ideas of center of mass, these results are not surprising. Given these results, we can evaluate the models if we have an independent measure of power, such as the Shapley-Shubik measure. Otherwise, they become, as they frequently have, simply a definition of power.

Third, we can evaluate the reasonableness of this class of models by a few general implications. Consider the basic characteristics of the simple force models:

1. There are a fixed number of known power sources.
2. At any point in time, each of these sources can be characterized as affecting the social choice by exerting force in terms of two dimensions, magnitude (power) and direction (initial position or behavior).
3. Any given source has a single, exogenously determined power. That is, power is constant (over a reasonable time period and subject-matter domain of observation) and always fully exercised.
4. The result (social choice) is some sum of the individual magnitudes and directions.

Insofar as the determinate models are concerned, both experimental and field observations make it clear that the models are not accurate portrayals of social choice. In order for the models to be accepted, the m_i (as defined in the models) must be stable. As far as I know, no one has ever reported data suggesting that the m_i are stable in a determinate model. The closest thing to such stability occurs in some experimental groups where the choices consistently come close to the mean, and in some highly formal voting schemes. In such cases, the power indices are occasionally close to stable at a position of equal power. Nevertheless, few students of power have claimed stability of the power indices.

When we move to the probabilistic case—or if we add an error term to the determinate models—the situation becomes more ambiguous. Since it has already been observed that rejection of a purely chance model is not too easy with the available data, the argument can be extended to models that assume significant error terms, or to models in which the number of observations is small enough to introduce significant sampling variation in the estimate of underlying probabilities. However, most observers of power in field situations are inclined to reject even such variations on the theme, although no very complete test has been made.

The basis for rejecting the simple force models (aside from the necessity of making them untidy with error terms) is twofold:

(1) There seems to be general consensus that either potential power is different from actually exerted power or that actually exerted power is variable. If, while potential power is stable, there are some unknown factors that affect the actual exercise of power, the simple force models will not fit; they assume power is stable, but they also assume that power exerted is equal to power. If actually exerted power is unstable, the simple force models will fit only if we can make some plausible assertions about the nature of the instability. For example, we can assume that there are known factors affecting the utilization of power and measure those factors. Or, we can assume that the variations are equivalent to observational errors with known distributions.

(2) There appears to be ample evidence that power is not strictly exogenous to the exercise of power and the results of that exercise. Most observers would agree that present reputations for power are at least in part a function of the results of past encounters. Although the evidence for the proposition is largely experimental, most observers would probably also agree that power reputation, in turn, affects the results of encounters. If these assertions are true, the simple force model will fit in the case of power systems that are in equilibrium, but it will not fit in other systems.

These objections to the simple force model are general; we now need to turn to models that attempt to deal with endogenous shifts in power and with the problem of power activation or exercise. As we shall see, such models have been little tested and pose some serious problems for evaluation on the basis of existing data. We will consider three classes of models, all of which are elaborations of the simple force models. The first class can be viewed as *activation models*. They assume that power is a potential and that the exercise of power involves some mechanism of activation. The second class can be described as *conditioning models*. They assume that power is partly endogenous—specifically that apparent power leads to actual power. The third class can be classified as *depletion models*. They assume that power is a stock, and that exercise of power leads to a depletion of the stock.

3.3 Force activation models

All of the models considered thus far accept the basic postulate that all power is exerted all of the time. In fact, few observers of social-choice systems believe this to be true, either for experimental groups or for natural social systems. With respect to the latter, Schulze argues that "the Cibola study appears to document the absence of any neat, constant, and direct relationship between *power as a potential for determinative action,* and *power as determinative action itself.*"[38] Wolfinger criticizes the reputational method for attributing power on the grounds that it "assumes an equation of potential for power with the realization of the potential."[39] And Hanson suggests that predictions based on the Miller-Form theory will be less accurate "when the issue does not arouse a high level of community interest and activity."[40]

As before, let m_{ij}^* represent the total power resources of the ith component at the jth choice, and let x_{ij} be the share ($0 \le x_{ij} \le 1$) of the total power resources that are exercised by the ith component at the jth choice. We associate the force activation models to the basic force models by means of the simple accounting expression

$$m_{ij} = \frac{x_{ij}\, m_{ij}^*}{\sum_{i=1}^{n} x_{ij}\, m_{ij}^*}.$$

We can consider two general variations on this theme:

The partition model. Suppose we let x_{ij} assume only two values, 1 and 0. That is, we assume that components in the system are either active or inactive on any particular choice. It is frequently suggested that power must be made relative to a specific set of actions or domain of joint decisions.[41] The specialization hypothesis is one form of such a model. We assume that once we have made the basic partition, we can treat the activated group as the total system and apply the basic force model to it.

The continuous model. Suppose we let x_{ij} assume any value be-

[38] R. O. Schulze, "The Role of Economic Dominants in Community Power Structure," *American Sociological Review,* XXIII (1958), 9.

[39] Wolfinger, "Reputation and Reality."

[40] Hanson, "Predicting a Community Decision."

[41] See H. A. Simon, "Notes on the Observation and Measurement of Political Power," *Journal of Politics,* XV (1953), 500–16; J. G. March, "An Introduction to the Theory and Measurement of Influence," *American Political Science Review,* LIX (1955), 431–51; March, "Measurement Concepts"; and R. A. Dahl, "The Concept of Power," *Behavioral Science,* II (1957), 201–15.

tween 0 and 1. That is, we assume that the participants in the system can vary their exercised power from zero to the total of their power resource. Thus, a relatively weak person can sometimes exert more power than a relatively strong one simply by devoting more attention to the choice problem involved.

Consider the problem of relating the activation models to observations of reality. Let us assume initially that potential power (m_{ij}°) is constant over all choices. We assume that there is something called *potential power* that is associated with a component of the choice system and that this power resource does not depend on the choice. In effect, this assumes that m_{ij}° is also constant over time, for we will require a time series of observations in order to make our estimates. We will relax this assumption in subsequent classes of models, but the constancy assumption is characteristic of most activation models.

Given the assumption of fixed potential power, we have two major alternatives. First, we can attempt to determine the value of x_{ij} for each component and each choice and use that information to estimate the potential power for each component. If we can determine by direct observation either the level of power utilization or the distribution of power utilization (or if we can identify a procedure for fixing the extent of utilization), we can estimate the potential power by a simple modification of our basic force models.

Suppose, for example, that we have some measures of the activation of individual members of a modern community. One such measure might be the proportion of total time devoted by the individual to a specific issue of social choice. We could use such a measure, observations of initial positions and social choices, and one of the basic force models to assign power indices (potential power) to the various individuals in the community. Similarly, if we took a comparable measure in an experimental group (e.g., some function of the frequency of participation in group discussions), we could determine some power indices. Because direct observational measures of the degree of power utilization are not ordinarily the easiest of measurements to take, the partition version of the model has an important comparative advantage from the point of view of estimation problems. Since we assume that the x_{ij} must be either 1 or 0, we need only observe whether the individual involved did or did not participate in a choice, rather than the degree of his participation.

If we are unable or do not choose to observe the extent of utilization directly, we can, at least in principle, estimate it from other factors in the situation. For example, if we can determine the opportunity costs[42] to the individual of the exercise of power, we might be able to assume that the individual will exercise power only up to the point at which the marginal

---

[42] See Harsanyi, "Measurement of Social Power, Opportunity Costs, ..."

cost equals the marginal gain. If we can further assume something about the relation between the exercise of power and the return from that exercise, we can use the opportunity costs to estimate the power of utilization. The general idea of opportunity costs, or subjective importance,[43] as a dimension of power has considerable intuitive appeal. If procedures can be developed to make the concepts empirically meaningful, they will be of obvious utility in an activation model of the present type. This route, however, has not yet attracted most persons doing empirical studies.

The second major alternative, given the assumption of constant potential power, is also to assume a constant utilization of power over all choices. Under such circumstances, the product $x_{ij}m^{*}_{ij}$ is a constant over all j. If both utilization and potential power are constant, we are back to the simple force model and can estimate the product $x_i m_i$ in the same way we previously established the m_i. Under such circumstances, the introduction of the concepts of power utilization and power potential is unnecessary and we can deal directly with power exercised as the core variable.[44]

The force activation model has been compared with empirical data to a limited extent. Hanson and Miller undertook to determine independently the potential power and power utilization of community members and to predict from those measures the outcome of social choices.[45] Potential power was determined by a priori theory; utilization was determined by inviews and observation. The results, as previously noted, were consistent not only with the force activation model but also with a number of other models. The French and Harary graph theory models are essentially activation force models (with activation associated with a communication structure) and they have been compared generally with experimental data for the equal potential power case. The comparison suggests a general consistency of the data with several alternate models. Dahl used a force activation model as a definition of power in his study of New Haven.[46] That is, he assumed the constancy of the x_{ij} and the m^{*}_{ij} within subject-matter partitions in order to estimate power. On the basis of other observations, Dahl, Polsby, and Wolfinger[47] seem to have concluded that it is meaningful to separate the two elements for certain special purposes (thus the classification as a force activation model rather than a simple force model). A New Haven test of the model, however, requires a subsequent observation of the stability of the indices.

[43] See R. Dubin, "Power and Union-Management Relations," *Administrative Science Quarterly,* II (1957), 60–81; and A. S. Tannenbaum, "An Event Structure Approach to Social Power and to the Problem of Power Comparability," *Behavioral Science,* VII (1962), 315–31.

[44] See Dahl, *Who Governs?* and Wolfinger, "Reputation and Reality."

[45] Hanson, "Predicting a Community Decision"; D. C. Miller, "The Prediction of Issue Outcome in Community Decision-Making," *Research Studies of the State College of Washington,* XXV (1957), 137–47.

[46] Dahl, *Who Governs?*

[47] Dahl, *Who Governs?* Polsby, "How to Study Community Power"; Wolfinger, "Reputation and Reality."

It is clear from a consideration both of the formal properties of activation models and of the problems observers have had with such models that they suffer from their excessive a posteriori explanatory power. If we observe that power exists and is stable and if we observe that sometimes weak people seem to triumph over strong people, we are tempted to rely on an activation hypothesis to explain the discrepancy. But if we then try to use the activation hypothesis to predict the results of social-choice procedures, we discover that the data requirements of "plausible" activation models are quite substantial. As a result, we retreat to what are essentially degenerate forms of the activation model—retaining some of the form but little of the substance. This puts us back where we started, looking for some device to explain our failures in prediction. Unfortunately, the next two types of models simply complicate life further rather than relieve it.

3.4 Force-conditioning models

The conditioning models take as given either the basic force model or the force activation model. The only modification is to replace a constant power resource with a variable power resource. The basic mechanisms are simple: (1) People have power because they are believed to have power. (2) People are believed to have power because they have been observed to have power. It is possible, of course, to have models in which one or the other of these mechanisms is not present. If we assume the first but not the second, we have a standard experimental paradigm. If we assume the second but not the first, we have an assortment of prestige learning models.[48]

Furthermore, it is clear that if power is accurately specified by observations and if social choices are precisely and uniquely specified by the power distribution, then the conditioning models are relatively uninteresting. They become interesting because of non-uniqueness in the results of the exercise of power or because of non-uniqueness in the attributions of power.

Let us assume that the C_j's are ordered according to the time of their occurrence. C_1 occurs immediately before C_2, and so on. Then we can view the general form of conditioning models as one of the basic force models as well as a procedure for modifying the m_{ij}^* as a consequence of the C_j. Consider, for example, the following model. We assume that the system reevaluates the power of the individual components after each choice. At that time, it has information on the choice (C_j) and the previous power reputations, $R_{j-1} = (r_{1, j-1}, r_{2, j-1}, \ldots, r_{n, j-1})$. It must assign a new set of power attributions, R_j. In assigning the new attributions, we might reasonably assume that the system affects the classic compromise of adaptive systems between (1) making the new solutions as consistent as possible with the immediate past experience, and (2) making the new solutions as

[48] White, "Uses of Mathematics in Sociology."

consistent as possible with the old solutions. In order to identify a dimension along which to affect this compromise, we define a minimum distance, $\overline{D}_j$, between the old attribution and the new choice: $\overline{D}_j = \overline{Q}_j - \overline{R}_{j-1}$, where $\overline{Q}_j$ is chosen so as to minimize

$$\sum_{i=1}^{n} (r_{i, \, j=1} - q_{ij})^2,$$

subject to

$$\sum_{i=1}^{n} q_{ij} A_{ij} = C_j.$$

We can define an equivalent form for the other basic force models.

Now we can assume $\overline{R}_j = \overline{R}_{j-1} + a\overline{D}_j$, where $0 \leq a \leq 1$. If a is 0, we have a degenerate case of a system that does not adapt. If a is 1, we have a system that always adapts the power reputations to be completely consistent with the past observations. If actual power does not depend on the perceived power and is constant, this system simply solves the set of equations (that is, learns the correct answer) or (in the case of the error elements) improves the estimates of power. Under these latter circumstances, it seems reasonable to assume that reputational techniques for assessing power will be preferable to direct observational techniques.

Our interest here, however, is in combining this mechanism with a second one, making actual power a function of perceived power. Within one of our basic force models (or an activation force model) we can define a reputation error, $e_{ij} = r_{ij} - m_{ij}$, and a simple form of adaptation, $m_{ij} = m_{i, \, j-1} + be_{i, \, j-1}$ where $0 \leq b \geq 1$. If b is 0, we have our constant power model. If b is 1, we have a model that adjusts power immediately to reputation.

Models of this general class have not been explored in the power literature. Experimental studies have demonstrated the realism of each of the two mechanisms—success improves reputation, reputation improves success. As a result, conditioning models cannot be rejected out of hand. Moreover, they lead directly to some interesting and relevant predictions.

In most of the literature on the measurement of power, there are two nagging problems—the problem of the chameleon who frequently jumps in and agrees with an already decided issue and the satellite who, though he himself has little power, is highly correlated with a high-power person. Since these problems must be at least as compelling for the individual citizen as they are for the professional observer, they have served as a basis for a number of strong attacks on the reputational approach to the attribution of power. But the problem changes somewhat if we assume that reputations affect outcomes. Now the chameleon and the satellite are not measurement problems but important phenomena. The models will predict that an association with power will lead to power. Whether the association is by chance or by deliberate imitation, the results are substantially the same.

To the best of my knowledge, no formal efforts have been made to test either the satellite prediction in a real-world situation, or to test some of its corollaries, which include:

1. Informal power is unstable. Let the kingmaker beware of the king.
2. Unexercised power disappears. Peace is the enemy of victory.
3. Undifferentiated power diffuses. Beware of your allies lest they become your equals.

Moreover, it is really not possible to re-evaluate existing data to examine the plausibility of conditioning models. Virtually all of the studies are cross-sectional rather than longitudinal. The data requirements of the conditioning models are longitudinal. They are also substantially more severe than for the basic force models. Consider the minimally complex adaptive model outlined above. We have added two new parameters (a and b) and a changing m_{ij} to our earlier estimation problems. In order to have much chance of using the model (or variants on it), we will probably need to have data on variables in addition to simply social choice and individual attitudes or behavior. For example, we will probably need reputational data. We will need data that is subscripted with respect to time. We will probably have to make some additional simplifying assumptions, particularly if we want to allow for probabilistic elements in the model or introduce error terms. I do not think these are necessarily insuperable problems, but I think we should recognize that even simple conditioning models of this type will require more and different data than we have been accustomed to gather.

3.5 Force depletion models

Within the conditioning models, success breeds success. But there is another class of plausible models in which success breeds failure. As in the conditioning models, we assume that power varies over time. As in the force activation models, we assume that not all power is exercised at every point in time. Thus,

$$m_{ij} = x_{ij} m_{ij}^\circ / \sum_{i=1}^{n} x_{ij} m_{ij}^\circ.$$

The basic idea of the model is plausible. We consider power to be a resource. The exercise of power depletes that resource. Subject to additions to the power supply, the more power a particular component in the system exercises, the less power there is available for that component to use. In the simplest form we can assume

$$m_{ij}^\circ = m_{i, j-1}^\circ - x_{i, j-1} m_{i, j-1}^\circ = m_{j, j-1}^\circ (1 - x_{i, j-1}).$$

And, if we assume that there are no additions to the power resources,

$$m_{ij}^\circ = m_{i, 0}^\circ (1 - x_{i, 0}) (1 - x_{i, 1}) \ldots (1 - x_{i, j-1}).$$

If the withdrawal rate is constant,

$$m_{ij}^* = m_{i,\,0}^* \, (1 - x_i)^j.$$

We can modify this to make the depletion proportional to utilization of power (rather than equal to it) without changing the basic structure of the model.

Under this scheme, it is quite possible for power to shift as a result of variations in the rates of power utilization. So long as additions to the power supply are independent of the exercise of power, the use of power today means that we will have less to use tomorrow. We can show various conditions for convergence and divergence of power resources or exercised power. We can also generate a set of aphorisms parallel to—but somewhat at variance with—the conditioning model aphorisms:

1. Formal power is unstable. Let the king beware of the kingmaker.
2. Exercised power is lost. Wars are won by neutrals.
3. Differentiation wastes power. Maintain the alliance as long as possible.

As far as I know, no one has attempted to apply such a model to power situations, although there are some suggestions of its reasonableness (at least as a partial model). Hollander has suggested a model of this class for a closely related phenomenon, the relation between the exercise of independence by a member of a group and the tolerance of independent behavior by the group; but his primary focus was on a system that involved, at the same time, systematic (but independent) effects on the resource (tolerance).[49] Some of the studies of interpersonal relations in organizations indicate that the exercise of power is often dysfunctional with regard to the effective exercise of power in the future. In those cases, the mechanism ordinarily postulated involves the impact of power on sentiments[50] rather than our simple resource notion. Nonetheless the grosser attributes of observed behavior in such studies are consistent with the gross predictions of models that view power as a stock.

Even if power resources are exogenous, the problems of testing a simple depletion model are more severe than the problems of testing the basic activation model. As in the case of the conditioning model, we require longitudinal data. Thus, if we can assume that power resources or increments to power resources are a function of social or economic status, skill in performing some task, or physical attributes (e.g., strength), the model probably can be made manageable if the simplifying assumptions made for force activation models are sensible. On the other hand, if we combine the depletion model with a conditioning model—as I think we probably ought to—

[49] E. P. Hollander, "Conformity, Status, and Idiosyncrasy Credit," *Psychological Review*, LXV (1958), 117–27.
[50] See W. G. Bennis, "Effecting Organizational Change: A New Role for the Behavioral Sciences," *Administrative Science Quarterly*, VIII (1963).

we will have complicated the basic force model to such a point that it will be difficult indeed to be sanguine about testing.

One way of moderating the test requirements is to use experimental manipulation to control some variables, and experimental observation to measure others. If we can control the resources available and directly measure the extent to which power is exercised, we can develop depletion and depletion-conditioning models to use in experimental situations.

If, however, we want to apply any of the more elaborate force models to a natural system, or if we want to develop natural-system predictions from our experimental studies, we will need far more data than recent research provides. Perhaps a model that includes considerations of activation, conditioning, and power depletion can be made empirically manageable, but such a model (and associated observations) would be a major technical achievement. We are not within shouting distance of it now.

Once we do get such a model, we may well find that it simply does not fit and that a new elaboration is necessary. From a simple concept of power in a simple force model, we have moved to a concept of power that is further and further removed from the basic intuitive notions captured by the simple model, and to models in which simple observations of power are less and less useful. It is only a short step from this point to a set of models that are conceptually remote from the original conception of a social-choice system.

3.6 Process models

Suppose that the choice system we are studying is not random. Suppose further that power really is a significant phenomenon in the sense that it can be manipulated systematically in the laboratory and can be used to explain choice in certain social-choice systems. I think that both those suppositions are reasonable. But let us further suppose that there is a class of social-choice systems in which power is insignificant. Unless we treat *power* as true by definition, I think that suppression is reasonable. If we treat *power* as a definition, I think it is reasonable to suppose there is a class of social-choice systems in which power measurement will be unstable and useless.

Consider the following process models of social choice as representative of this class:

An exchange model. We assume that the individual components in the system prefer certain of the alternative social choices, and that the system has a formal criterion for making the final choices (e.g., majority vote, unanimity, clearing the market). We also assume that there is some medium of exchange by which individual components seek to arrange agreements (e.g., exchanges of money or votes) that are of advantage to themselves. These agreements, plus the formal criterion for choice, determine the social decision. This general type of market system is familiar enough for economic systems and political systems.[51] It is also one way of viewing some modern theories of interpersonal influence[52] in which sentiments on one dimension ("I like you") are exchanged for sentiments on another ("You like my pots") in order to reach a social choice ("We like us and we like my pots").

A problem-solving model. We assume that each of the individual components in the system has certain information and skills relevant to a problem of social choice, and that the system has a criterion for solution. We postulate some kind of process by which the system calls forth and organizes the information and skills so as systematically to reduce the difference between its present position and a solution. This general type of system is familiar to students of individual and group problem solving.[53]

A communication-diffusion model. We assume that the components in the system are connected by some formal or informal communication system by which information is diffused through the system. We postulate some process by which the information is sent and behavior modified, one component at a time, until a social position is reached. This general type of system is familiar to many students of individual behavior in a social context.[54]

A decision-making model. We assume that the components in the system have preferences with respect to social choices, and that the system has a procedure for rendering choices. The system and the components operate under two limitations:

1. Overload: They have more demands on their attention than they can meet in the time available.
2. Undercomprehension: The world they face is much more complicated than they can handle.

Thus, although we assume that each of the components modifies its behavior and its preferences over time in order to achieve a subjectively satisfactory combination of social choices, it is clear that different parts of the system contribute to different decisions in different ways at dif-

---

[51] See, for example, Anthony Downs, *An Economic Theory of Democracy* (New York: Harper & Row, Publishers, 1957); J. M. Buchanan and Gordon Tullock, *The Calculus of Consent* (Ann Arbor: University of Michigan Press, 1962); and Riker, *The Theory of Political Coalitions.*

[52] Dale Carnegie, *How to Win Friends and Influence People* (New York: Simon and Schuster, Inc., 1936); Leon Festinger, *A Theory of Cognitive Dissonance* (New York: Harper & Row, Publishers, 1957).

[53] See, for example, A. Newell, J. C. Shaw, and H. A. Simon, "Elements of a Theory of Human Problem Solving," *Psychological Review,* LXV (1958), 151–66; and D. W. Taylor, "Decision Making and Problem Solving," in *Handbook of Organizations,* ed. March.

[54] See, for example, Elihu Katz and P. F. Lazarsfeld, *Personal Influence* (New York: Free Press of Glencoe, Inc., 1955); and Angus Campbell, Philip Converse, W. E. Miller, and Donald Stokes, *The American Voter* (New York: John Wiley & Sons, Inc., 1960).

ferent times. This general type of system is a familiar model of complex organizations.[55]

In each of these process models, it is possible to attribute power to the individual components. We might want to say that a man owning a section of land in Iowa has more power in the economic system than a man owning a section of land in Alaska. We might want to say that, in a pot-selling competition, a man with great concern over his personal status has less power than a man with less concern. We might want to say that a man who knows Russian has more power than a man who does not in a group deciding the relative frequency of adjectival phrases in Tolstoi and Dostoievski. Or, we might want to say that, within an organization, a subunit that has problems has more power than a subunit that does not have problems. But I think we would probably not want to say any of these things. The concept of power does not contribute much to our understanding of systems that can be represented in any of these ways.

I am impressed by the extent to which models of this class seem to be generally consistent with the reports of recent (and some not so recent)[56] students of political systems and other relatively large (in terms of number of people involved) systems of social choice. "Observation of certain local communities makes it appear that inclusive over-all organization for many general purposes is weak or nonexistent," Long writes. "Much of what occurs seems to just happen with accidental trends becoming commulative over time and producing results intended by nobody. A great deal of the communities' activities consist of undirected cooperation of particular social structures, each seeking particular goals and, in doing so, meshing with the others."[57]

Such descriptions of social choice have two general implications. On the one hand, if a system has the properties suggested by such students as Coleman, Long, Riesman, Lindblom, and Dahl, power will be a substantially useless concept. In such systems, the measurement of power is feasible, but it is not valuable in calculating predictions. The measurement of power is useful primarily in systems that conform to some variant of the force models. In some complex process systems we may be able to identify subsystems that conform to the force model, and thus be able to interpret the larger system in terms of a force activation model for some purposes. But I think the flavor of the observations I have cited is that even such

[55] See C. E. Lindblom, "The Science of Muddling Through," *Public Administration Review,* XIX (1959), 79–88; and R. M. Cyert and J. G. March, *A Behavioral Theory of the Firm* (Englewood Cliffs, N.J.: Prentice-Hall, Inc., 1963).

[56] For example, David Riesman, *The Lonely Crowd* (New Haven: Yale University Press, 1951).

[57] N. E. Long, "The Local Community as an Ecology of Games," *American Journal of Sociology,* XLIV (1958), 252.

interpretations may be less common-sensible than we previously believed.[58]

On the other hand, the process models—and particularly the decision-making process models—look technically more difficult with regard to estimation and testing than the more complex modifications of the force model. We want to include many more discrete and nominal variables, many more discontinuous functions, and many more rare combinations of events. Although some progress has been made in dealing with the problems, and some predictive power has been obtained without involving the force model, the pitfalls of process models are still substantially uncharted.

4.0 THE POWER OF POWER

If I interpret recent research correctly, the class of social-choice situations in which power is a significantly useful concept is much smaller than I previously believed. As a result, I think it is quite misleading to assert that, "Once decision making is accepted as one of the focal points for empirical research in social science, the necessity for exploring the operational meaning and theoretical dimensions of influence is manifest."[59] Although *power* and *influence* are useful concepts for many kinds of situations, they have not greatly helped us to understand many of the natural social-choice mechanisms to which they have traditionally been applied.

The extent to which we have used the concept of power fruitlessly is symptomatic of three unfortunate temptations associated with power:

Temptation No. 1: The obviousness of power. To almost anyone living in contemporary society, power is patently real. We can scarcely talk about our daily life or major political and social phenomena without talking about power. Our discussions of political machinations consist largely of stories of negotiations among the influentials. Our analyses of social events are punctuated with calculations of power. Our interpretations of organizational life are built on evaluations of who does and who does not have power. Our debates of the grand issues of social, political, and economic systems are funneled into a consideration of whether i has too little power and j has too much.

Because of this ubiquity of power, we are inclined to assume that it is real and meaningful. There must be some fire behind the smoke. "I take it for granted that in every human organization some individuals have more influence over key decisions than do others."[60] Most of my biases in this regard are conservative, and I am inclined to give some credence to the utility of social conceptual validation. I think, how-

[58] See Bachrach and Baratz, "Two Faces of Power."
[59] March, "An Introduction," p. 431.
[60] R. A. Dahl, "A Critique of the Ruling Elite Model," *American Political Science Review*, LII (1958).

ever, that we run the risk of treating the social validation of power as more compelling than it is simply because the social conditioning to a simple force model is so pervasive.

Temptation No. 2: The importance of measurement. The first corollary of the obviousness of power is the importance of the measurement problem. Given the obviousness of power, we rarely re-examine the basic model by which social choice is viewed as some combination of individual choices, the combination being dependent on the power of the various individuals. Since we have a persistent problem discovering a measurement procedure that consistently yields results which are consistent with the model, we assert a measurement problem and a problem of the concept of power. We clarify and re-clarify the concept, and we define and redefine the measures.

The parallel between the role played by power in the theories under consideration here and the role played by subjective utility in theories of individual choice is striking. Just as recent work in power analysis has been strongly oriented toward conceptual and measure-ment problems, so recent work on utility theory has been strongly oriented toward conceptual and measurement problems.

Although I have some sympathy with these efforts, I think our perseveration may be extreme. At the least, we should consider whether subsuming all our problems under the rubric of conceptual and meas-urement problems may be too tempting. I think we too often ask *how* to measure power when we should ask *whether* to measure power. The measurement problem and the model problem have to be solved simultaneously.

Temptation No. 3: The residual variance. The second corollary of the obviousness of power is the use of *power* as a residual category for explanation. We always have some unexplained variance in our data—results that simply cannot be explained within the theory. It is always tempting to give that residual variance some name. Some of us are inclined to talk about God's will; others talk about errors of ob-servation; still others talk about some named variable (e.g., power, personality, extrasensory perception). Such naming can be harmless; we might just as well have some label for our failures. But where the unexplained variance is rather large, as it often is when we consider social-choice systems, we can easily fool ourselves into believing that we know something simply because we have a name for our errors. In general, I think we can roughly determine the index of the temptation to label errors by computing the ratio of uses of the variable for pre-diction to the uses for a posteriori explanation. On that calculation, I think power exhibits a rather low ratio, even lower than such other problem areas as personality and culture.

Having been trapped in each of these cul-de-sacs at one time or another, I am both embarrassed by the inelegance of the temptations involved and impressed by their strength. We persist in using the simple force model in a variety of situations in which it is quite inconsistent with observations. As a result, we bury the examination of alternative models of social choice under a barrage of measurement questions.

I have tried to suggest that the power of power depends on the extent to which a predictive model requires and can make effective use of such a concept. Thus, it depends on the kind of system we are confronting, the amount and kinds of data we are willing or able to collect, and the kinds of estimation and validation procedures we have available to us. Given our present empirical and test technology, power is probably a useful concept for many short-run situations involving the direct confrontations of committed and activated participants. Such situations can be found in natural settings, but they are more frequent in the laboratory. Power is probably not a useful concept for many long-run situations involving problems of component-overload and undercomprehension. Such situations can be found in the laboratory but are more common in natural settings. Power may become more useful as a concept if we can develop analytic and empirical procedures for coping with the more complicated forms of force models, involving activation, conditioning, and depletion of power.

Thus, the answer to the original question is tentative and mixed. Provided some rather restrictive assumptions are met, the concept of power and a simple force model represent a reasonable approach to the study of social choice. Provided some rather substantial estimation and analysis problems can be solved, the concept of power and more elaborate force models represent a reasonable approach. On the whole, however, power is a disappointing concept. It gives us surprisingly little purchase in reasonable models of complex systems of social choice.

FOUR

TALCOTT PARSONS
Harvard University

The Political Aspect
*of Social Structure and Process**

This paper will present, in exceedingly condensed form, an approach to the theoretical analysis of political structure and process. The approach owes much to many analyses and discussions in the tradition of political theory; it is distinctive largely in that it places such materials in the context of a general theoretical analysis of the total society as a social system.[1]

Our key orienting concept is the *polity,* defined as a primary functional subsystem of a society, strictly parallel in theoretical status to the *economy,* as that concept is broadly used in modern economic theory.[2] The term *functional* here means that the polity should not be identified either with any specific collectivity structure within the society, such as government

---

* In the preparation of this paper I am particularly indebted to Victor M. Lidz, who helped in shaping the argument itself through numerous discussions, mobilized reference material, edited the manuscript for style and clarity, and adapted the Technical Note from its previous use (appended to "On the Concept of Political Power").

[1] See the appendix for an outline of the relevant highlights of this theory.

[2] See Talcott Parsons and N. J. Smelser, *Economy and Society* (New York: Free Press of Glencoe, Inc., 1956); N. J. Smelser, *The Sociology of Economic Life* (Englewood Cliffs, N.J.: Prentice-Hall, Inc., 1963); and P. A. Samuelson, *Economics: An Introductory Analysis,* 5th ed. (New York: McGraw-Hill Book Company, 1961).

71

(any more than the economy should be conceived as the aggregate of business firms), or with any concrete type of activity of individuals. It is conceived analytically as the aspect of all action concerned with the function of the collective pursuit of collective goals. The collectivity in question may be any system involving the coordinated action of a plurality of individuals oriented to the attainment of a collective goal or a system of collective goals. Collectivities in this sense range from very small groups to the political aspect of what Roscoe Pound called the "politically organized society,"[3] most notably the "state," and beyond that, to intersocietal organizations.

A *collective goal* here means a relatively optimal relation between the collectivity and some aspect of its intrasocietal situation (e.g., other collectivities) or its extrasocietal environment. It may concern relations not only to other collectivities, but also to personalities of individuals, cultural objects (e.g., as a result of change through research), and organic or physical objects. Especially for a collectivity continuing in time and holding multiple interests, a particular goal is not isolated; it is part of a system of goals. Any particular goal must, therefore, be fitted into a larger system of goals, according to its rank-order and timing with reference to other goals. A *goal* exists only if the desired state differs from the actual or expected state at the inception of action. Goals admit of degrees of attainment, all-or-none instances being special cases.

Committing a collectivity to attain a goal implies, in addition to an assertion of the desirability of the goal's attainment, a commitment to relatively specific measures designed to effect the desired goal-state. Hence, it involves the mobilization of resources at the collectivity's disposal, through authorized agencies. Thus, commitment to the attainment of a collective goal implies resource commitments which, under the pressure of conditions, themselves require further decision-making processes.

The attainment of its goal by a collectivity is, in the paradigmatic, integrated case, the performance of function to the social system of which it is a part (the system includes structures other than goal-oriented collectivities). The proposition that such operations are "on behalf" of the larger system therefore assumes an "adequate" degree of integration of the larger system. Short of such integration, one must allow for structural dislocations which may cause a "success" from the viewpoint of the collectivity to constitute malfunction from the viewpoint of the system. Nevertheless, I wish to assert the fundamental proposition that collectivities are always the *agencies* of specific performances of societal function. Persons in roles perform functions in (and for) collectivities, but not directly in total social systems. The alleged performance of social goal-attainment function by an individual, e.g., an "independent" artisan or professional practitioner, is in

---

[3] In seminars at Harvard University.

fact the limiting, single-member case of a collectivity, a "corporation sole." The performance of societal function by "informal cooperation" without formal collectivities is another limiting case, one that minimizes the factor of "organization."

Like all other functional activities in social systems, political action must be regulated in terms of a value-standard.[4] The concept of *effectiveness* as used by Barnard fills the requirements of the value-standard very exactly.[5] It is directly parallel to *utility* as used in economic theory. If commitment to the collective goals may be considered as given, at the relevant levels, political judgment must concern the probability that implementive measures will in fact bring about the desired changes; that is, one must judge whether the available resources are adequate and the organization of their use competent. Here, effectiveness is the standard according to which the measures are evaluated. Insofar as the structures and processes of the polity are differentiated from those of the other societal subsystems, its value-standard will be also.

The distinction between effectiveness and utility involves complex questions which cannot be treated here. However, political effectiveness is parallel at the level of social organization to technological effectiveness at the level of physical production. Thus, cost in the economic sense is only one of several considerations involved in judgments of effectiveness. Whether or not resources devoted to a given collective goal might be better devoted to some alternative use cannot be determined on economic grounds. Such grounds are relevant to deciding whether or not to make commitments to a goal, but are irrelevant to evaluating the effectiveness vis-à-vis the situation and environment of measures undertaken to attain the goal. Cost, then, is not a political category itself, although it is relevant at the economic level and, as such, is conditional to political decisions. Cost is also relevant, at a cybernetically higher level, to the integration of the social system of which the political unit is a part, even if the unit comprises the total society in its political aspect. Here, cost is involved in choices among both the goals of a given collectivity and, for the wider system, the goals of its various collectivities. In this case, however, cost is integrative, not economic. It refers to the sacrifices in system-solidarity entailed by commitment to one collective goal as compared with the sacrifices entailed by commitments to alternative goals. In one context, this cost may be assessed in terms of the sacrifice of political support risked by those taking responsibility for collective decisions. In another context, it may be stated in terms of possible changes in the level of commitment to general collective action—that is, of loyalty to the social system in question.

[4] Talcott Parsons, "On the Concept of Political Power," *Proceedings of the American Philosophical Society*, CVII, No. 3 (1963), 232–62.

[5] C. I. Barnard, *The Functions of the Executive* (Cambridge: Harvard University Press, 1938), esp. pp. 236–39.

Before discussing the principal components of political structure and process, we must consider another central concept—*bindingness,* a quality of commitments and decisions which is both a condition of effective implementation of policies and a mode of specification of the value-standard of effectiveness.[6] As political process is a process of collective goal-attainment, it involves making decisions with regard to the implementation of the collectivity's values in relation to situational exigencies. For that implementation to be effective, the decisions regarding it must, to give assurance to the objects in the social situation,[7] be *binding* on the collectivity and, hence, on any member-units bearing responsibility for contribution to the implementation process. By virtue of membership, member-units may be regarded as having assumed certain very general commitments to contribute to collective processes. In the present context, decision making may be considered a process which specifies these generalized commitments so that, in a specific situation, specific units are expected to do or not to do specific things. *Bindingness* thus links these two levels of commitment.

The concept of *bindingness* is also central to the problem of sanctions.[8] If commitments or obligations exist and, as may be assumed for theoretical purposes, are acknowledged by the relevant members of a collectivity, questions will arise sooner or later about what consequences an obligated actor must face if he makes known his intention not to fulfill what the agent responsible for implementation considers his obligation. Whatever the extenuating circumstances, no system can be indifferent about the fulfillment of such an obligation. In cases of threatened noncompliance, the activator of the commitment may be expected to insist on compliance, as it indeed is generally his obligation to do. In cases of continuing noncompliance, insistence inevitably includes the threat of imposing negative sanctions as a consequence of noncompliance. Then their implementation becomes a com-

[6] Parsons, "On the Concept of Political Power."

[7] This implies that in action systems, situational goal-objects are typically "social objects" having expectations in some sense complementary to those of the collectivity of reference. These social objects are either collectivities sharing membership in the same social systems or individuals in roles. In either case, attainment of the collective goal cannot be considered "secure" unless, in reciprocation with the social objects, binding obligations are assumed by the collectivity, for *its* interests are dependent on the objects' complementary performances. There are two principal limiting cases in which such complementarity fails to hold. First is the case of physical objects which by definition have no expectations in the action sense. A technologically oriented organization will be actuated in relation to physical materials and equipment by considerations of cost, not of obligation to the physical objects. Second is the "sovereign" collectivity which relates to other collectivities without any normative order. Clearly this is never the empirical state of affairs in an "international" system; it is a limiting concept.

[8] See Talcott Parsons, *The Social System* (New York: Free Press of Glencoe, Inc., 1951), Chapter Seven, for a general discussion of the importance of sanctions.

mitment of the threatener.[9] As will be made clear later, this in no way implies that fear of negative sanctions is the principal motive for honoring collective commitments. But it does imply that contingent negative sanctions are inherent components of the political system, because without them it would be senseless to insist on the bindingness of commitments.[10]

Like any social system, a political system is structurally composed of units and their relationships. As every political system is a collectivity, its units are always "members" which may be either individual persons *in roles*[11] or subcollectivities which themselves are ultimately reducible to individual persons in member roles. Member-units are characterized by four essential properties:

1. Generalized commitments to the specific values of the collectivity, i.e., their commitment to the collectivity's effectiveness, which may be called their loyalty;
2. Specified commitments consisting of rights and obligations to make certain types of decisions which integrate the collectivity's commitments with their own roles and statuses within it;
3. An integrative responsibility for implementing specified decisions and protecting certain interests of the collectivity, a responsibility which constitutes a normative context for particular roles or functions; and
4. A capacity to implement, through instrumental procedures, decisions constituting obligations in particular roles. Capacity includes both competence in the personal sense and control of resources adequate for specific purposes.

Since effectiveness is a value-pattern for a collectivity, ideally all members should be equally committed to it as a value on the generalized level. Empirically, however, there are both variations of intensity of commitment,

[9] To take a simple case, most voluntary associations which require dues have a rule that those who persistently and intentionally fail to pay the dues will have rights of membership revoked. The responsible officers cannot simply ignore intentional nonpayment indefinitely. At some time, they must honor their commitment to enforce the rules if the association is to function effectively in this respect.

[10] In the present context, any change in the situation which an enforcing agent can impose, and which is disadvantageous to the units from whom performance of commitments is expected, may serve as a negative sanction. Physical force has a strategic place in negative-sanction systems which is based on a special relation to territoriality; but that cannot be discussed here. See my "Some Reflections on the Place of Force in Social Process," in *The Problem of Internal War,* ed. Harry Eckstein (Princeton: Princeton University Press, 1963).

[11] The qualification *in roles* is essential, because no one, after early infancy, is ever a member of only one collectivity. The expression "*x* is a member of *y* association" is correct; but it is elliptical because it does not specify the other collectivities to which *x* also belongs. There have been spurious implications that the total person, not the "portion" of him involved in a specific role, is a member of a specific collectivity, often "society" almost personified.

and alienation in the sense of conflict over commitment, including complex ambivalences.

The operative functions of collective process tend to be structured primarily around the second and fourth of the above properties of membership roles. Specified commitment is very close to what is often called the operative member's *sphere of responsibility*. Integrative responsibility, however, involves an additional component. It goes beyond responsibility in a clearly defined status to include a share of responsibility for defining the status.

THE CONCEPTS OF AUTHORITY AND OFFICE

The primary institution carrying such relational responsibility in political function may be called *authority*. The unit-status associated with it may be called *incumbency of an office*.[12] Here I take the radical position that the concept of office should apply to *all* membership statuses in a collectivity. Thus, all such statuses are statuses of authority and, by that virtue, all members have some degree of power. Rather than differentiating between those having and those lacking authority and power, the more useful approach is to distinguish between those who have relatively more and those who have relatively less authority and power. Thus, to take an important case, voting membership in an association is here considered a position of authority, an office, and the franchise, though it has little power under the principle of one member, one vote, most definitely *is* power—just as a single dollar, though not much money, certainly *is* money.

Authority, then, is the legitimated right to make certain categories of decisions and bind a collectivity to them. Authority may be held not by an individual but by a collegial body, a subcollectivity such as a committee, in which individual members have only the authority to cast votes contributing to collective decisions.

There are two main kinds of authority, each of which is essential to collective functioning. The first, which is more purely political, regards the position of the office in a hierarchy of decision-making priorities. The second, which articulates with nonpolitical factors, concerns the "functional" areas within which authority operates.

Collective effectiveness depends on capacity to coordinate the actions of diverse contributing units and assure with bindingness that each will do its part. There must, then, be a priority scale among the *rights* to make decisions which, in a manner sufficiently differentiated to cope with the complexity of the organization, places those by which the collectivity is bound to specific policies above those by which various commitments are undertaken to effect policy implementation. Such an institutionalized priority scale of decision-making functions is the hierarchy of authority we have

[12] See Max Weber, *The Theory of Social and Economic Organization* (New York: Free Press of Glencoe, Inc., 1947), pp. 329 ff.

designated as an essential component of collectivity structure. Its structural principle seems to be a ratio scale. Thus, authority is arranged on a series of levels such that a status at a higher level of authority will take a precedence, structured in the manner of a proportion, over all lower statuses with reference to rights of decision making over the allocation of available resources. A particular scale along which such precedence relations are structured is a line of authority in the classical sense.

Collective effectiveness, however, also depends on adaptation to the qualitatively diverse exigencies to which collective operations are subject, both those exigencies situational to it and those involved in capacities and motives of member-units on whose contributions the collectivity relies. These exigencies are necessarily differentiated with respect to both their inherent properties and their functions in collective processes. The principle of hierarchy is, therefore, crosscut by the principle of functional differentiation as it has a bearing on implementive effectiveness. Thus, the collectivity must be divided into departments, divisions, etc., with each being assigned responsibility for a more-or-less differentiated aspect of operations.

Matters are further complicated because functional differentiation is not one-dimensional. It may be based on several different principles. For example, a collectivity with extensive operations may often be segmented territorially into branch offices with different locations; it may also be differentiated on such bases as specialization in particular technological processes. These are, of course, familiar complications regarding bureaucratic organization, which is one of the main types of structural complex in political systems, according to the present conception.[13]

The essential modifications of the hierarchical principle involved in bureaucratic (implementive) systems may be derived from the boundary exigencies of the system as expressed in qualities of the inputs necessary for collective processes. Here, one must distinguish the collective or political system from the technical system. The latter carries out technological processes and therefore is both the agency of manipulation of physical processes and the consumer of physical goods. The political system, however, controls the technical system.

This distinction greatly simplifies the definition of political exigencies bearing upon the implementive context, as it reduces them to the securing of financial resources and human services. Financial resources give access to *all* kinds of concrete resources accessible through the market. These concrete resources can be reduced to the two basic classes: goods and services.[14]

The critical problem here concerns the relation of resources to the

[13] Talcott Parsons, *Structure and Process in Modern Societies* (New York: Free Press of Glencoe, Inc., 1960), Chapters One and Two.
[14] For present purposes, "cultural objects," as resources, can be assimilated into these two categories if we speak of the "embodiment" of cultural meanings in physical objects, such as books, or in services, such as copyrights, and their "internalization" in persons, as in the form of technical competence.

category of membership. Only human agents, individual or collective, can be *units in* a collective system. Money is a means of procuring services. In one context, by giving money to the performer of a service, the employing collectivity enables him to satisfy his wants, for example, in his capacity as family member. In another context, money constitutes the budget for facilities enhancing the performer's work within the collectivity, whether they are at the disposal of his role or whether higher echelons spend them for the benefit of his role. Such facilities constitute a primary component of the "opportunity for effectiveness" which the agent receives in accepting employment in a collectivity instead of working on his own.

In return for this opportunity, the employee typically gives the collectivity rights to control his actions in the context of employment. The critical element to the collectivity is the right to ensure with binding power that his action contributes effectively to collective goal-attainment. A primary source of the power which the collectivity's leadership uses and allocates through the hierarchy of authority is the aggregate of commitments to service made by units who have accepted employment in the collectivity. Such commitments are initially generalized, defined only by the terms of the "job"; over time, they are continually specified to the many particular tasks undertaken and performed as occasions arise.

A crucial fact is that the authority of all offices stops at the boundary of the collectivity of reference. Therefore, in a sufficiently differentiated system, employment need not impair the freedom of the employee's personal actions outside the collectivity. In a free labor market, potential performers of service have, before actually accepting employment, no obligations of performance. Hence, the agent of the employer cannot insist that they perform, but may only negotiate to acquire their consent and, with that, their obligations to accept direction.[15] Hence, the labor market performs fundamental functions in setting the boundary of the authority-hierarchy, especially by defining certain limits within which that hierarchy is confined. Among the terms settled in a contract of employment is the position the employee will occupy in the hierarchy, including its risks and opportunities. His status may vary from the lowest menial position to chief executive.

This boundary makes an adjustment between grant of authority or power, and capacity and acceptance of responsibility for contribution. This boundary relation is thus governed, not by hierarchy of authority, but by opportunity to acquire positions in the hierarchy of authority, an opportunity which tends in turn to be governed by equality of units under universalistic standards of selection, the only principle maximizing collective effectiveness in the long run.

---

[15] This may, of course, be incompletely institutionalized, e.g., in transition periods, so that abuses may develop. See N. J. Smelser, *Social Change in the Industrial Revolution* (Chicago: University of Chicago Press, 1959).

THE CONCEPT OF POWER

I have used the term *power* a number of times. Now it is necessary to define it more explicitly and precisely.[16] I conceive *power* to be a generalized symbolic medium which circulates much like money, the possession and use of which enables the responsibilities of an office with authority in a collectivity to be more effectively discharged. *Authority* is the politically crucial quality of a status in a social structure. Power I conceive, in contrast, to be a primary instrumentality of effective performance *in* that position. To be effective, a unit must have an income of power, must be willing to spend it, and yet must be prudently rational in doing so. This may involve either transferring power to other units within a collectivity or transferring it over the collectivity's boundaries.

Power may be regarded as a medium for controlling action which, under certain conditions, is exchangeable for other such media operating in contexts from which power is excluded. The two other media we must now consider are money and influence. Money is a linear continuum which may be appropriately divided in terms of cardinal quantities; the question of "how much" is always essential in monetary contexts. For power, which is ordered in terms of a ratio scale, the question is not how *much* power does someone have, but what his position is *relative* to other foci of decision making. Furthermore, in a sense not necessarily applicable to money, the scale of positions with regard to power must be *particular* to the collectivity of reference and its boundaries. Universalistic principles, then, operate only in reference to access to power, influence on power, or standards governing the use of power.

Monetary resources can be allocated in a quantitative and distributive sense, as a pie can be divided into equal or unequal slices. Power-allocation, however, also involves questions of both the degree and the field of delegation. One does not divide power into numerically fractional shares, but one does decide which levels and spheres in a system are to be held by whom. Opportunity for effectiveness provides a distribution context for power, and is differentiated on the two axes, "level" in the power hierarchy and functional type of unit-contribution.

Delegation of power or authority is performed as an exchange for something of value that consists of facilities for effective implementation of collective goals. A classification of types, then, must derive from the differentiation of the factors which enter into effective collective functioning. On the administrative or implementive side, the crucial factor is control of economic productivity, primarily through financial resources, which in turn is the basic condition for securing services. To attract services, however, the organization must, in addition to paying money, offer opportunity for effec-

16 See Parsons, "On the Concept of Political Power."

tiveness through position in both the hierarchical and qualitatively differentiated aspects of the power system. Although connected, these aspects vary independently. Indeed, freedom to alter the qualitative combinations "lower down" is a critical hierarchical feature of executive authority in this context. However, a primary condition of adequate integration of a collectivity is a good match in hierarchical position and functional location between the delegated power held by occupational members and the capacities which employed units bring to the organization.[17]

Because it relates to the bindingness of obligations, any use of power must, as noted, also relate to legitimized coercive sanctions. The free labor market, however, introduces a limiting factor which impinges primarily on higher authority. Not only acceptance of membership through employment, but also its continuation is voluntary in principle. Leaving the collectivity by resigning is always in principle a possibility. Thus the grant of power to the collectivity is conditional and can always be withdrawn. The consent of the employed to the discipline imposed upon him is hence a condition of retaining his services.[18]

This consensual condition to the attraction and retention of service relates to the functional significance of certain freedoms regarding the organizational role. Particularly important are roles that involve high levels of technical competence. Such competence is necessarily specialized, whereas high levels of authority in a collectivity necessarily involve responsibility for relatively wide ranges of problems. A person of high *technical* competence, therefore, is not likely to have an *organizational* superior who can competently judge the technical quality of many of his decisions—only his professional peers can do so. The specialist must, then, be given freedom from intervention by authority within his technical sphere. Yet, in order to be effective in attaining collectively desired outcomes, his specialized operations must be coordinated with other operations within a collective organization—hence he ordinarily has no interest in going it alone. The price of opportunity is acceptance of the organization's authority system within certain limits. Typically, the organization can effectively hold him responsible for satisfactory results, but not for the technical ways in which he achieves them. Collective responsibility for the technical and ethical standards governing such matters must lie predominantly with a professional association

[17] Discussion in this context of *alienation* sometimes fail to make a critical distinction. In the economic context, the *alienation of labor* may be understood as the sacrifice of self-sufficiency in production in favor of advantages gained from the division of labor. In the political context, we may speak of the *alienation of services* which gives an employing collectivity *power* to control the manner of contribution to collective functioning. Perhaps the latter is the primary component of "alienation of labor" in the Marxian sense.

[18] There are important exceptions to this voluntary principle. Those in a deviant status, such as prisoners and the committed mentally ill, constitute one type. The closest to the occupational role is military service where, even when enlistment is voluntary, resignation at will is ordinarily not permitted.

which crosscuts the many types of operative organization employing its members.

By the nature of power systems, such expenditures of power by delegation must be balanced by incomes of power, essentially in the form of consent to accept organizational authority. The effective power, as distinguished from the authority, of an organizational status depends upon the aggregate of action commitments of organizational members to perform services within the sphere of the status-incumbent's responsibility. His possession of power typically depends on their voluntary continuance in their respective appointive positions.[19] The process complementing delegation of power may, then, be called its *aggregation,* in that a plurality of power "quanta" must be aggregated as the power income of a position. They will be differentiated according to both hierarchical level and the qualitative sphere of the assumed obligations.

Some Limitations of Bureaucratic Structure

The aspect of political structures just outlined is usually called the *bureaucratic* or *administrative subsystem,* which is concerned primarily with the implementation of collective goals. For territorially organized societies, these goals typically include the maintenance of the basic internal order and the defense of territorial integrity, however gradually this may shade into aggression. They also include the mobilization of resources, in the case of government largely through taxation, for maintaining the administrative establishment as well as the differently structured components of the collective structure. Of course, there generally are various other goals, in the governmental case, especially the maintenance of such public functions as religious cults and priesthoods and welfare and economic policies.

One of Weber's famous dicta was that the top of a bureaucratic structure cannot itself be bureaucratic.[20] He specifically associated this with the problem of legitimation. Because it is a subsystem of a society, a polity can not be self-legitimating. It must depend for legitimacy on institutionalized values and agencies bearing primary responsibility for them, such as religious collectivities. Here the place of the valuation of collective effectiveness in the wider institutionalized value system is critical. In the American case, for example, it is far from having the highest priority. Generally, we favor autonomy of units over the subordination of units to collective interests. Hence, at the governmental level we emphasize the maintenance of limitations on the authority of government, e.g., through the Bill of Rights. The Soviet Union leans much further toward giving collective effectiveness top priority.

[19] Cf. Barnard's concept of efficiency of cooperation, in his *Functions of the Executive,* esp. pp. 253–55.
[20] Weber, *Theory of Social and Economic Organization,* p. 335.

Legitimation, then, functions to define what political organization is for and, hence, to define the nature and scope of the agencies—collectivities and roles—which perform political functions. Correlative with these structural definitions are both authority for the implementation of the legitimate responsibilities, and access to power and the conditions of its use. In a sufficiently differentiated polity, we call this *the constitutional system*—with private as well as public collectivities having constitutions more or less formally specified. Where the political aspect of social structure is sufficiently differentiated from the others, *all* authority is "rational-legal" in Weber's sense.[21] His two other types of authority occur where structural differentiation is relatively incomplete. It is possible to link Weber's, or a more developed typology of authority, to a general typology of stages in the differentiation of the functional spheres of social systems.[22] Space limits my discussion to a few outstanding points.

A critical question here concerns the extent to which the constitutional definition of political authority is legally formulated and then institutionally interpreted by legal agencies essentially independent of executive and even legislative authorities, and of the trusteeship of the value-maintenance agencies.[23] Lack of differentiation from the sphere of value-maintenance is typical of systems of religious law, like those of Islamic societies, which give the civil normative system direct religious sanction. Lack of differentiation from the sphere of executive and legislative authorities is typical of early modern absolutism, in which the monarch claimed the prerogative to define the legal nature and limits of his own authority, subject only to religious sanction. Thus Justice Coke's ultimately successful assertion of the independence of the law from the royal prerogative in England was a landmark.[24] Such independence is, indeed, a major criterion of the polity's differentiation from other societal subsystems, notably from what I call *the pattern-maintenance system*. For private collectivities, legal definition of authority and other rights is largely, though not entirely, imposed from outside. Clear reasons for this are abundant. For example, private corporations cannot simply arrogate to themselves rights and prerogatives that either conflict too drastically with those claimed by public authority or vary too greatly from those enjoyed by similar corporations. This is one reason that the universalistic characteristics of advanced legal systems are most im-

---

[21] Weber, *Theory of Social and Economic Organization*, p. 328.

[22] Talcott Parsons, "Evolutionary Universals in Society," *American Sociological Review*, XXIX (June, 1964), 339–57; Talcott Parsons, *Societies: Comparative and Evolutionary Perspectives* (Englewood Cliffs, N.J.: Prentice-Hall, Inc., 1966).

[23] Max Weber, *Max Weber on Law in Economy and Society* (Cambridge: Harvard University Press, 1954), esp. Chapter Eleven.

[24] See David Little, "The Logic of Order: An Examination of the Sources of Puritan-Anglican Controversy and of Their Relations to Prevailing Legal Conceptions of Corporation in the late 16th and Early 17th Century in England" (Doctoral thesis, Harvard University, 1963).

portant—e.g., the American Constitution's prohibition of bills of attainder, or, especially prominent now, the doctrine of "equal protection of the laws."

In another context, the legitimation subsystem of large-scale political systems has been differentiated only recently from what I call the *support system*. The absolutist regimes ascribed the obligation of political support to the status of subject, as indeed modern totalitarian regimes do. Differentiation is marked by the development of legitimized procedures for expressing opposition to current leadership without impunging one's loyalty to the system. This implies that there are legitimized procedures for changing leadership, and that various constituent elements may try to bring about such change.

THE SUPPORT SYSTEM

In a differentiated support system, the leadership's "constituency" constitutes a democratic association. The franchise is the institutionalized instrumentality for giving support or nonsupport to specific leadership groups. Support systems are assumed to be hierarchical structures which are parallel to, and articulate with, the hierarchy of bureaucratic structures. There is an uneven distribution of the authority to make decisions that bind the association as a collectivity and, hence, its members in their respective roles. There is, to be sure, a theoretical limiting case where there is equally distributed power, but it requires that every decision be made by majority vote of the membership in order to be binding. This becomes more difficult to maintain as the scale, complexity, and urgency of collective business increase. Hence, parallel to the delegation of authority in bureaucratic systems, support systems, operating within constitutionally defined terms, grant authority and power to elected leadership subject to electoral defeat, i.e., withdrawal of support, as defined by procedural rules.[25]

Despite the many variations in the nature and extent of the franchise, there are certain relatively uniform tendencies in its institutionalization. A first essential is the establishment of procedural institutions which are reliably accepted across lines of internal conflict on policy matters. The severest test of these institutions comes when an incumbent leadership is expected to relinquish power after its electoral defeat. Since, in the case of the state, with its great control of resources and coercive machinery, this is a severe test indeed, it is not surprising that such institutions fail so often.

Aside from such reliance on formal procedural institutions, Rokkan[26] has shown that three other elements of the franchise also tend to develop in democratic polities. First is universal adult suffrage. Thus, property and sex

[25] See Talcott Parsons, " 'Voting' and the Equilibrium of the American Political System," in *American Voting Behavior,* eds. Eugene Burdick and Arthur Brodbeck (New York: Free Press of Glencoe, Inc., 1959).

[26] Stein Rokkan, "Mass Suffrage, Secret Voting, and Political Participation," *European Journal of Sociology,* II (1961), 132–52.

qualifications, to say nothing of religious ones, have generally been eliminated in Western electoral systems. Second is equality of the franchise. Class systems, in which votes are weighted unequally, tend to be eliminated; the last flagrant example of a class system was the Prussian one which was abolished at the end of World War I. In effect, however, markedly unequal apportionment of legislative seats relative to population often has some qualities of a class system. The Georgia county-unit system, invalidated by the U.S. Supreme Court in Gray v. Sanders in 1963, was an example. Third is secrecy of the ballot, which helps to differentiate the voting role from a member's other personal roles, thus protecting the freedom of his vote from pressures exerted by status superiors and peers.[27]

From the above, it is evident that a crucial characteristic of support systems, and hence democratic associations, is a relatively clear definition of membership status, especially of the boundary between membership and nonmembership. For the politically organized society, membership involves citizenship, the prerogative of which is the enjoyment of civil rights, including the franchise. There must therefore be distinctions between citizens and aliens, the latter enjoying fewer civil rights (e.g., being denied the franchise). The correlates of civil rights, of course, are such obligations as taxation and military service, and, in general, compliance with the policy decisions of duly constituted authority.

The franchise in a democratic association, public or private, is a form of authority, and its exercise is power because the decision of an electorate is strictly binding on the collectivity; defeated incumbents must relinquish their offices to new leaders. Election to office is a power input to the leadership of the polity, enabling it to exercise or spend power in making policy decisions which commit collective resources to specific uses and in delegating opportunity for effectiveness to members of the administrative system. Here, as in other contexts, power has an hierarchical aspect which stands in a complex and important relation to an egalitarian aspect. The hierarchical aspect takes an all-or-none form from the election. Just as one is, or is not, a citizen and endowed with power through the franchise, so one is, or is not, elected to office. The power of office is not divided among candidates according to the proportion of votes they received; all of it is given to the one elected.[28]

---

[27] I have recently argued elsewhere that both bureaucratic organization and democratic association are universals in social evolution in that their successful development generalizes adaptive capacity in degrees essential to the emergence of fully modern societies. These propositions are further explained in my "Evolutionary Universals in Society."

[28] Proportional representation systems are not an exception to this statement. Seats may be allocated according to proportions of party votes, but a given candidate is, or is not, elected. No proportional system goes so far as to elect candidates to represent their constituents on percentages of the issues coming before the legislature corresponding to the proportions of the votes they received.

Commonly, we think of democratic associations as inherently egalitarian and of power systems as inherently hierarchical, and so altogether dissociate membership and the franchise from power. This contradicts my view that the franchise is directly a form of authority and that its exercise is a form of power. The link between franchise and hierarchy lies in the aggregation of votes to determine electoral victory—that is, the difference between being in and out of office. Though the victor in an election becomes hierarchically superior to the loser, all the voters who determine the outcome may still be equal in regard to the power of their votes.

Power in a collectivity is a means of effectively mobilizing obligations in the interest of collective goals. Modifications of hierarchy involved in the employment of bureaucratic services are boundary-interchange conditions that differentiate the occupational role of the individual from his private concerns—a matter strongly stressed by Weber.[29] Unless the status of employment is either ascribed or coerced, it is necessary to offer inducements. In doing so, the employer cannot assert an hierarchical precedence based upon his internal authority. As stated in very general form above, he must use inducements consisting of opportunity for effectiveness and of monetary reward. Regarding the return for such inducements, the egalitarian element of equality of opportunity enters because the offer of concrete opportunity is conditioned on competence (that is, expected contribution to effectiveness).

We have emphasized that, as a function of the differentiated institutionalization of associational collectivities, the boundary between membership and nonmembership tends to become more clearly defined. There are of course various components of membership status, but the franchise seems to be crucial, since it is the component of the power of government of the association which is linked to membership as such. Subject then to such exceptions as minority and legal "incompetence" to manage one's own affairs, there tends to be a rigid distinction between members who enjoy the franchise and nonmembers who do not, with a strong tendency to institutionalize the principle of one member, one vote.

The relevant all-or-none principle then extends to the selection of leadership in that, once a set of offices in an association have been set up, it is essential to know *who* the legitimate incumbent is, since he exercises power in a representative capacity on behalf of and *binding on the collectivity*. It is this functional exigency, representation of and bindingness for the collectivity as a whole, which explains the application of the all-or-none principle to election to office. If the powers of office were divided according to the strength of electoral support, as measured by votes, the representation would be that of "interests," not of the collectivity as a whole. For executive office the implication seems clear. For the legislature it is somewhat different in that legislators are representatives of their constituencies, in which

[29] Weber, *Theory of Social and Economic Organization*.

some interest components will be, relative to the system as a whole, more salient than others. A legislator, however, at the same time has, by his vote in the legislature, a share of power to bind the total collectivity. In this connection he must, in order to make his action binding on a constituency as part of the whole, be in a position to legitimize the bindingness of the consequences of his vote on members of his constituency who were *not* of the predominant persuasion within it. The constituency is thus not only an "interest group," but also a genuine *segment* of the total political system.

The boundary distinction between membership and nonmembership is thus directly parallel in the case of citizenship status with that of employment in an "administrative" collectivity. In both cases one is either in or out; the cases of intermediate status are marginal. The same is true of the all-or-none principle as applying to what is usually called office within the collectivity, in the sense of the incumbent being given power to bind the collectivity as a whole, at the level and in the sphere of the "jurisdiction" of his office. The one essential difference lies in the procedure of access to office; in the administrative context it is appointive, while in the associational context it is elective.

In both cases there is an element of hierarchy in the structure of offices and their powers. Here again, it is common features of the exigencies of effectiveness in collective goal-attainment which account for the hierarchical component. The essential reference is again to bindingness for the collectivity as a whole. The diversity of interests which will somehow come to be involved in any complex collectivity is such that the "right" to make binding decisions cannot be dependent on any specific momentary and probably unstable combination of such interests, but must be independent of them. At the same time, the more "parochial" the level of operation of official authority, the more likely it is that interests particular to the subsystem of reference will exert strong pressure to decide "their way." If unitary responsibility is to be achieved, once the purely "populist" solution of deciding every issue by full membership vote has become impossible, there must be a hierarchy of offices in the sense that conflicts at lower levels must be resolvable by referring decisions to "higher authority." Of course it is the crucial feature of a democratic association that the highest elected official agency, president, or even legislature, is held responsible by the membership as a whole in that the power acquired by election is revocable through electoral defeat.

Power systems we conceive to be strictly bounded by membership status; the more so, the more differentiated is the polity from other societal subsystems. A society, however, consists of a large plurality of politically organized collective units, extending all the way from the societal community and its government to nuclear families. A crucial aspect of the pluralism of modern social structure lies in the fact that typical units, individuals and subcollectivities, have membership status in a considerable number of political collectivities. The mechanism of influence operates not only to help to persuade members and office-holders within any one collectivity of reference to make the decisions with reference to the use of power desired by the exerter of influence, but also to articulate the grounds for, and evaluation of, the consequences of particular decisions in particular units of the polity with the policies of other units in the broader system. Indeed, the use of influence within a politically organized collectivity may be said to be to an important degree a mechanism of adjustment of the relations of its subcollectivities with each other.

Thus government has tended to a territorial focus of organization. But in the American system, as in other federal systems, there has been an important measure of autonomy institutionalized for territorial subunits. Insofar as states' rights have been institutionalized, coordination among the states has had to rely on influence at least as much as the direct use of power. The salience of conflicts in this area should not blind us to the importance of the positive possibilities of influencing the power-holders in states to "cooperate" in the national interest, even beyond the reach of the federal power in the literal sense. The same principles apply at the level of local autonomy and "home-rule" vis-à-vis both state and federal power.

Power as a generalized medium would not be necessary if the decisions of collectivities could be arrived at solely by the *quid pro quo* of political barter—"You vote for my measure, and I'll vote for yours." Power, we have argued, becomes necessary in giving representatives power vis-à-vis their constituencies—especially the minorities in them who are yet bound by their representatives' votes—and again giving the outcome of legislative votes binding character for the collectivity as a whole. Were the outcome a matter of pure political barter, there *could* be no dissident minorities whose cooperation either had to be "coerced" at the level of reaching the collective decision, or at least was made voluntary in part by their loyalty to the collectivity at a more general level.

At the next more general level of scope of interests and normative considerations, the integration of the many subcollectivities in a complex social system, notably a society, is achieved in a parallel sense by the mechanism of influence. Still less than in the power context would it be conceivable here for such integration to be achieved through barter alone, i.e., the trading of "interests" without their guarantee by binding authority. A very large part of the use of influence goes to persuading interest-spokesmen to accept binding obligations. In the context of government this refers us to the *consensus* aspect. It is probably the case that the more differentiated the society, the less possible it is for government to operate successfully without the backing of the informal consensus (or "loyalty") of most of the membership of the relevant societal community. Such loyalty, however, will only operate when it can be assumed that important elements are willing to trust leadership *beyond* the level of their formal commitments in terms of authority and power.

In its relation to the support system, hierarchy is still a function of the imperatives of collective effectiveness. The power output from the leadership elements of a collective organization to their constituencies consists of the responsibility those elements take for policy decisions. Within the constitutional framework, these decisions specify already established, highly generalized goals and establish priorities among various subgoals; thereby, collective commitments to specific subgoals and then measures for their implementation are made. A basic difference between the bureaucratic and associative contexts is that policies are open to decision making by associative leaders, whereas administrators are obliged to implement policies already established, even though they may also be expected to give "feedback" as to what future policies seem desirable from their viewpoint. Although, as is so generally the case, empirical lines are difficult to draw, this seems to be the crucial analytical distinction.[30]

Concretely, the process of policy decision has a dual character. It is the basis of the directives which policy-makers give to the administrative agencies responsible to them. It is a process internal to the polity. But it is also a process of power output from the polity to its constituencies through the support system. Thus, the power acquired from constituents in the electoral process is returned through another boundary interchange between the polity and the contiguous subsystem of the society, the integrative system.

We interpret this aspect of policy decision as an output of power to the community, which is conceived of as composing the constituencies of elective office. The crucial feature of this aspect of policy decision is the bindingness of policy decisions on all elements obligated to the collectivity as either associational or bureaucratic members. Policies, however, impinge differentially, not equally, on members. They generally favor certain interests over others and impose varying obligations so that they somewhat reallocate resources.

Such differential impingement must be justified with reference to the legitimation of both the paramount goals of the collectivity and of the rights of leadership to make such decisions.[31] Policy decisions essentially spell out

---

[30] Concretely, of course, administrative agencies make policy, e.g., through administrative interpretation of a legislative act or executive order. Just as clearly, however, their primary function is not policy making; and the primary function of elected officials and their immediate advisers is not administration. It is a question of primacy.

[31] I include both executive and legislative elements here in the category of leadership. Like all such distinctions within our scheme, it is mainly functional in the last analysis. The legislative responsibility here is interpreted to be the formulation—or ratification—of the most general levels of policy and of the broad rules for their implementation. The executive function seems to center on modes and timing of implementation with, of course, responsibility for referring sufficiently broad problems to the legislative agency. The legislative func-

in more detail the primary goal commitments of a collectivity as specific situations develop and as their exigencies change. Unless the system is very undifferentiated, there must be mechanisms for justifying more particular decisions *within* the framework of the standards that provide legitimation. These I interpret as centering in the relations between power and influence as mechanisms for mediating social processes and the system's normative structure. In one context, justification refers to a consensual reference of the power system. When used to make policy decisions, power is presumptively justified so long as it remains within the limits of legitimate authority and adheres to the accepted norms. There is, however, a second, more specific aspect of justification, which has to do with the positions of the subgoals in the hierarchy which situationally specify the more general goals of the collectivity, and with the interests served by commiting resources to those subgoals.

Here, however, inherent integrative problems arise. Resources are inherently scarce relative to demands for their use; and benefits and obligations are differentially distributed to interest groups. To resolve these grounds of conflict two basic factors are needed: persuasion that the relevant subgoal is urgent for the collectivity as a whole and persuasion that shifts in the benefit-burden balance implied by the decision are fair. For collective leadership, this involves exercising influence relative to the important elements of the constituency by "taking responsibility" for the implications of the decision, even at the risk of losing future political support. In a reasonably stable system, this output of influence may be conceived of as balancing the influence exercised by "interest groups" during the decision-making process.

These statements require support by a brief account of the concept of *influence*.[32] I conceive *influence* to be a generalized medium of social interaction that circulates among social units in the context of persuasion. It operates neither by offering situational inducements, such as economically valuable commodities, services, or money, nor by promulgating binding decisions backed by conditional, coercive sanctions, as in the use of power. Influence operates entirely on the intentions of the object of persuasion and through positive channels. It tries to convince him that acting as the persuader desires is in his own and the collective interest.

The major "intrinsic" means of persuasion is to declare firm intentions to act in ways favoring the particularistic interests or senses of solidarity held by specific segments of the constituency. Such persuasion is common and important, but it is theoretically analogous to barter in the case of economic exchange. It is insufficiently generalized to cover the vast gaps which

---

tion in democratic states is concentrated in parliaments and congresses, but in less than fully democratic associations it is performed primarily by fiduciary boards to which the executive agencies are in some sense responsible.

[32] Talcott Parsons, "On the Concept of Influence," *Public Opinion Quarterly,* XXVII (1963), 37–62.

arise in complex systems between the interests in ensuring support for policies and the necessity for decision making that can cope with situational exigencies, when the constituencies are characterized by differentiation of functions, religious, ethnic, and social pluralism, and diversity of space-time locations.

If the declaration of specific intentions, the effect of which is to establish solidarity in some kind of a "coalition" with the object of persuasion, is the barter prototype of the exercise of influence, the medium itself operates at a higher level of generality, not the declaration of specific intentions, but rather of support for the more general "objectives" of the object of persuasion. Here the essential point is the establishment of solidarity and a contribution to its operation, without immediately specifying just *what* goals or interests are to be actively supported, e.g., the election of a particular candidate to a particular office, or the promulgation of a specific policy decision.

Influence is of course, under certain circumstances, in institutionalized systems as defined by procedural rules, convertible for power. Thus when President Johnson and Vice-President Humphrey declared in favor of Comptroller Beame for Mayor of New York, they were exerting influence, which the Beame group hoped would be converted into power in the form of votes. Johnson and Humphrey did not in any clear sense "control" blocs of votes in the New York City election, but their general positions of prestige in the Democratic Party were hoped to serve as a generalized means of persuading Democratically inclined voters—however ineffectual it proved in the particular case.

Influence, then, I conceive of as the medium of persuasion which relies not on acceptance of the intrinsic argument presented, but on the prestige or reputation of the source of the argument. Like money and power, influence, to be sound, must ultimately be exchangeable for the intrinsically valuable inputs for which it is an appropriate medium. This fact, however, does not diminish the importance of its use *instead of* intrinsic means in many circumstances, for as we have noted, a complex polity could not operate on a basis of political barter. If support of leadership depended solely on deals regarding specific policy decisions, it would be very constricted. Unless support is ascribed to particular aspects of leadership status, such as hereditary class status, or to qualities of leadership transcending the political function, such as religious charisma, a generalized medium must be used to transcend barter and naked power in aggregating support.

It is also clear that in modern societies ascriptive bases of mutual obligation or expectation will operate constrictively. For the administration of a large-scale organization to be effective, the resources—especially the human resources—of the organization must be highly mobilizable. Inducements through the market can fill an important part of this need, but there are limits to the use of monetary advantage which cannot be transcended by the use of power. Here, influence may be utilized to persuade holders of resources, including their own services, that it is in their own long-run interests, financial and otherwise, to take certain actions, such as accepting a particular kind of occupational role. Political processes in modern totalitarian societies of the Soviet variety tend to blur the distinction between such uses of influence and appeal to the moral obligations involved in commitment to the regime. This moralism of expecting everything for the party and "building socialism" tends readily to become a basis for coercion.[33]

I will discuss influence with the other generalized media below in connection with some general problems of analyzing political process. Here, however, I will use this sketchy outline of its characteristics to examine Rokkan's conclusion that electoral systems inherently develop toward equality of the franchise. This problem is particularly salient because, if one holds that voting is an exercise of power, then the equality of the franchise strikingly contrasts with the hierarchical element in bureaucratic and leadership systems of power, the element very generally regarded as their defining characteristic. The solution of this problem may be found in the relations among power, influence, and the normative justifications of their use.

The value-premises of the relevant institutions concern the individualism in the value-system I have called *instrumental activism*.[34] According to this value-pattern, a ramified social system contains, rather than an over-all system goal, a set of standards for determining the social acceptability of goals of the system's units. From the viewpoint of the society, this is the value-basis of goal pluralism. From the individual's viewpoint, the basis is the valuation of both his autonomy and the absence of discriminations among individuals which are not justified by exigencies which the concrete system must meet in order to implement the values.

Such exigencies justify two basic grounds for limiting complete autonomy and nondiscrimination. First, the normative order must contain a compulsory element to protect the system from disruptions by force and fraud. Second, equal responsibility for policy decisions is incompatible with the conditions of collective effectiveness, for reasons stated above. Hence, power is concentrated in elective offices.

Subject to these two sets of conditions, the ideal patterns of the assumed value-premises are freedom of association, so that acceptance of membership obligations is as nearly voluntary as possible, and equality of the power of membership status as such, as distinguished from that of particular offices. The electoral system links these two patterns by aggregating the equal votes to determine the incumbency of offices and policy decisions on matters referred to the membership in referendum. Because the burden of proof falls on contentions that the goals of certain individual members will yield par-

[33] See Gregory Grossman, "The Structure and Organization of the Soviet Economy," *Slavic Review*, XXI (1962), 203–22.

[34] I cannot take space here to explain fully these statements about values. For the American case, the fullest statement is Talcott Parsons and Winston White, "The Link Between Character and Society," in *Culture and Society*, eds. S. M. Lipset and Leo Lowenthal (New York: Free Press of Glencoe, Inc., 1961). A much fuller analysis will be published later.

ticularly valuable social contributions, there is no ground for discriminating among individuals regarding the amount of power inherent in membership.

However, it is manifestly impossible for all goals proposed by individuals or subgroups to have equal value and prospect for implementation. It is, then, as a mechanism for selecting and ordering the goals or interests of individual members and subcollectivities and the binding policies of the collectivity that influence is most significant politically. Individual members must be *persuaded* (not coerced or induced) to vote for candidates and policies; and office-holders must be *persuaded* to make policy decisions desired by their constituents. Justification of such decisions must be based on the more or less universalistically ordered normative system.

The institutions of franchise and elective office operate together to regulate, in broad accord with the paramount values, the distribution and use of power and the distribution of resources and obligations resulting from the use of power. In the long run, the quality of such regulation depends upon the solidity of the differentiation between power and influence. Here, problems focus about protecting voters from coercion as they exercise the franchise—they must be persuaded genuinely—and protecting office-holders from illegitimate pressure on the part of interest groups.

The conception, held by many eminent writers, that power is governed only by hierarchical principles clearly depends on the idea that the political system of reference is a closed system.[35] It is at the polity's two critical boundaries, however, that its most essential modifications appear. If, as I have argued, opportunity for effectiveness is power, then the principle of equality relative to competence governs a major access to power, however imperfectly this is realized in practice. It is crucial here to link the concept of service, as a category of the output of economic processes, to consideration of the bureaucratic or administrative aspect of collective organization. When freedom of the individual's choice has been institutionalized, the exigencies of procuring services necessitate the basic modification of hierarchical principles which is found at this boundary. At the boundary of membership (in the sense of the constituency of leadership), the hierarchical principle is modified even more radically by the principle of equality of the franchise. This, I have suggested, results from the exigencies of securing consent to the selection of leadership and to policy decisions.

DIFFERENTIATION OF POLITICAL STRUCTURES

These considerations have an important bearing on the broad understanding of political structure; they refer particularly to the key concept of

---

[35] V. O. Key, *Politics, Parties, and Pressure Groups*, 4th ed. (New York: The Crowell-Collier Publishing Co., 1958); H. D. Lasswell and Abraham Kaplan, *Power and Society* (New Haven: Yale University Press, 1950); and R. A. Dahl, *Modern Political Analysis* (Englewood Cliffs, N.J.: Prentice-Hall, 1963).

collectivity. The focus of the political aspect of a social system is organization oriented to the attainment of collective goals. This organization is subject to three primary sets of exigencies.

The first concerns the legitimation of collective goals and of the authority and power needed to implement them in terms of the values of the wider social system, not those of its political subsystem. The wider value-patterns must be specified as commitments in the context of collective action along the requisite lines and subject to the requisite limitations. The legitimation subsystem of a highly differentiated polity, therefore, centers about the constitutional system and the judicial agencies which interpret it. This subsystem is a major link between political and legal organization and thereby involves the integrative structures of the society. Any concrete collectivity depends on fulfillment of these functions, however rudimentary the agencies which implement them may be. The judicial branch of the U.S. government is a highly differentiated example.

Secondly, a political system is an agency for mobilizing resources from its intrasocietal environment and utilizing them to implement its policies. This is the function of the bureaucratic subsystem within which organization based on hierarchical "line authority" is most clearly differentiated. This principle, however, is sharply modified at the boundary where needed resources or capacities can be brought into the polity only by inducement and can be controlled by authority only through the intervention of influence.

Thirdly, there is the associational subsystem. This mobilizes not implementive resources, but rather constituent support and determination of the policies to be implemented. Such mobilization involves the interplay of power and influence between leadership and membership, the latter having dual roles as constituents and as interest groups.

This duality is, in a certain sense, parallel to the duality of roles of the members of households in relation to economic production through the market system. On the one hand, they are consumers, the source of primary market demand for goods. On the other hand, they are in the labor force and, as such, candidates for employment. Taken together, these two markets are the main boundary zones between the economy and its "final" production. Similarly, political leadership and the decision making of office have a dual relation to the publics which are associationally related to them. These publics constitute the sources of demands for particular policy decisions and, as such, function as interest groups. Some of the same people are also the sources of political support, above all, but not exclusively, through voting. The roles, however, must be distinguished, for where support is sufficiently generalized, it is not directly exchanged for particular policy decisions—that would be the political equivalent of barter. Another medium is needed to bridge the gap between the two "markets." This medium we conceive to be influence.

When the associational component dominates the others, we speak of *an association,* as in the case of a professional association of scientists. When the bureaucratic component is clearly primary, we generally do not call the collectivity *an association.* The typical manufacturing firm is such a case. Associational members have the passive role of stockholders, while their leaders, the boards of directors, are often almost assimilated into the top management. Authoritarian governments also approximate this type, although the top of the bureaucracy can never be purely bureaucratic. Independent collectivities giving clear primacy to the legitimation subsystem are far less prominent among political structures, although some types of religious organization do fit that category.

To conclude this sketch of the structure of political systems—which, one must remember, applies to both public and private collectivities—I will briefly discuss the principal ranges of their variability. So far I have emphasized the variability deriving from functional differentiation not only in the polity itself, but also in its relations to the other societal subsystems.

We have conceived the bureaucratic subsystem to be differentiated primarily in relation to economic exigencies, namely the procurement and management of the more-or-less fluid resources at the polity's disposal, and the corresponding outputs of political benefits. The critical resources are, first, financial, and, second, the services of individuals and collectivities. In a developed system, physical resources are mediated by these factors. The associative subsystem is differentiated with respect to problems of support, and outputs of policy decision are differentiated with respect to the management of influence inputs and outputs. Finally, the legitimation subsystem is differentiated with respect to relationship between the polity and the general normative structures (value-patterns and legal norms) of the society.

These external references of the polity's structural differentiation relate very closely to its internal differentiation, which I will treat here only briefly.[36] Very roughly, I will designate four primary internal subsystems of the polity.

In the analytical sense of this paper, a political system is by definition characterized by the primacy of commitment to the attainment of collective goals. Hence there should be a special primacy of the goal-attainment subsystem, which is not a quality of all types of social systems. In the broadest terms, this subsystem may be called the "leadership" subsystem; its spearhead—the more highly differentiated the system, the more so is the "politically responsible executive," whether, as in the American national system, a popularly elected president, or, in the parliamentary type, a prime minister and cabinet directly responsible to the legislature. This responsible executive is "flanked" within the leadership system on the one hand (the

---

[36] The scheme I would present, were there space, would follow the model for the economy introduced by Smelser and myself in *Economy and Society,* Chapter Four, further developed by Smelser in *Social Change in the Industrial Revolution.*

adaptive) by those who are mainly responsible for implementing executive policies, but not as such the highest order of decision-makers. These are the chief executive's "executive staff" which may involve cabinet members and administrative staff in varying combinations. On the other hand (the integrative) are those elements which constitute the principal liaison between executive and legislature, which is here conceived to involve the *dual* role of sponsors of the principal interest groups in the system, and direct involvement in the main system of collective responsibility. Legislative leadership stands most intimately in interchange with the executive in this sphere. The relatively "inert" pattern-maintenance subsystem of the leadership system is perhaps best described as the set of commitments of the whole leadership cohort to the values of the political system as a whole, to effectiveness, but effectiveness within the framework of the more general societal value-system and its political constitution. The very highest level functions of the judiciary might be conceived to fit here.

Just as the executive component of leadership is "flanked" on two principal sides, it may be suggested that the leadership sector as a whole is similarly flanked. On the adaptive side is the administrative system which is ordinarily referred to as the "bureaucracy." The center of gravity here is in the elements which do not carry policy-making authority. Their functions are primarily implementive rather than originating. That no absolutely clean concrete line can be drawn does not change this general distinction.

On the integrative side, the leadership system as a whole must articulate with its basis in the integrative functions of the polity as a whole. In modern political systems, this seems to be broadly shared between legislative and judicial functions. The legislative gives relatively specific support, which takes the form of power, to the leadership—in parliamentary systems the whole position of the leadership depends directly on this. The judicial system gives a broader framework of justification and legitimation to the trends of leadership. Of course, on occasion, lack of judicial legitimation or justification may be very serious to leadership policies.

The legitimation of the whole political system as agency of the collectivity is the primary function of the pattern-maintenance subsystem of the polity. It rests in the first instance on its constitutional position and the constitutional framework within which its main orientations fit. The formal legal constitution, however, never stands alone, but has a background of more diffuse commitments in the societal community as a whole. Thus, the "American Creed," with reference to race relations, recently exerted pressure on the Constitution, in the first instance through the Supreme Court, rather than vice versa.

One range of variation among polities concerns the stage of differentiation of a given empirical polity with regard to both its differentiation from the other societal subsystems and its internal differentiation. Obviously, the two are closely interdependent.

The most primitive societies, as Lowie long ago made clear,[37] certainly have political functions, notably because of territorial exigencies. But they typically have no differentiated political structures which are not concurrently structures of kinship involving other primary functions. The early or "archaic" empires made no clear structural distinctions between the political and the religious components of their governmental structures. From such diffuse structures, bureaucratic aspects tend to be differentiated earliest; then comes some sort of independent legal system. A democratic electoral system finally emerges, but it remains the most difficult to institutionalize, with the problems involved varying considerably relative to its size.[38]

Another range of variation, though not so primary as that of differentiation, certainly needs to be mentioned. It concerns the levels at which given normative patterns are effectively institutionalized. For instance, British society seems not to carry certain aspects of differentiation between the polity and the other aspects of social structure as far as the United States does; thus, Britain has, for example, that aspect of social stratification known as the "Establishment." At least until recently, however, the British polity has probably been on its own terms more fully institutionalized than ours, so that phenomena like McCarthyism have been less likely to appear in Britain.[39]

SOME ASPECTS OF POLITICAL PROCESS

From the present theoretical viewpoint, social process in sufficiently differentiated systems is centered in interactive exchanges involving the generalized symbolic media. In other words, the centrality of monetary transactions in economic analysis is used as a model for political and other sorts of analysis. For the political case, the focal medium is power. At various points in the societal system, power is exchanged both for other generalized media, notably money and influence, and for intrinsically significant rewards (services and support) and factors of effectiveness. Factors of effectiveness, at levels where they are not primary symbolic media of social systems, include the technological means of effective coercion and administration, and the like, many of which must be mobilizable with money funds. At higher levels in the normative hierarchy of control, the intrinsic means of political process are commitments to collective loyalty and the value-commitments underlying them.

[37] H. Lowie, *The Origin of the State* (New York: Harcourt, Brace & World, Inc., 1927).

[38] I cannot take space here to treat this enormous field any further. For a modest systematization of such material, see my *Societies, Comparative and Evolutionary Perspectives*.

[39] See my "Social Strains in America" and S. M. Lipset, "The Sources of the Radical Right," *The Radical Right* (Garden City, N.Y.: Doubleday & Company, Inc., 1963).

In analyzing processes involving the symbolic media, three types of process should be distinguished. Again following economic models, they may be called *circular flow,*[40] *growth,* and *structural change.*

Circular flow

No social system, perhaps least of all a polity, functions in a completely stable environment. Of the three components of the polity's intrasocietal situation, the legitimation system is presumably the most stable. It is difficult to generalize about the relative stability of the economic and integrative boundaries, but both are ordinarily less stable than the legitimation boundary. In other words, in any complex and differentiated political system, administrative and policy problems continually arise and change.

The primary function of power in *this* context is to stabilize the polity in the face of changes in its environment. Essentially, the process is always one of translating generalized expectations into more specific ones. Responsible leadership obviously cannot predict in advance the specific actions that exigencies will require of their collectivity if its generalized effectiveness is to be maintained. Without precise knowledge of situational and environmental conditions, leadership cannot even define the goals which appear to be most attractive in terms of the generalized collective commitments. Hence it cannot impose situationally adapted obligations on its members far in advance of actual developments. But, lacking knowledge of what goals and means of implementation will be involved in future actions, responsible leadership can use its generalized power to allow for contingencies by holding open freedoms of choice which never emerge in ascriptive conditions, and which are exceedingly awkward to manage in barter conditions. Thus, the user of power can specify political obligations to levels of performance which were left undefined when the general undertaking began—e.g., in making an employment contract or in giving political support to a leadership element.

Without balancing mechanisms, however, such degrees of freedom would produce instability. The essential feature of the balancing mechanisms is feed-back from the condition of resource scarcity. In the case of power, however, the scarcity element does not concern expenditure of a given fraction of a cardinal quantity, as it does with money, but the capacity to carry the day in establishing or implementing decisions as binding. The hazard of overspending is that losing on important issues will impair capacity to prevail in others. Such impairment, provided that it is not so radical as to jeopardize legitimation, involves three primary factors.

The first is the risk that power inputs balancing such expenditures will not be forthcoming. Thus, failures in effective administration (through fail-

[40] See Joseph Schumpeter, *The Theory of Economic Development* (Cambridge: Harvard University Press, 1936).

ure to procure or hold qualified services, for example) may lead to withdrawal of political support. Hence, there is a balance in the economy of power itself, a balance which is effected in quantum steps rather than in an even flow. Good administration and policy making should "make" power, as well as secure intrinsically significant results, just as production "makes" both goods and money for the producing unit.

Over the long run, the balance-of-power potential depends upon capacity to exchange power for the media of the societal subsystems adjacent to the polity. Hence, inadequate financial resources, whether procured through taxation, market transactions, or solicitation of voluntary contributions, comprise a second type of factor in the impairment of political processes. As Eisenstadt points out, when feudalization shrinks the base of mobilizable resources, e.g., taxes, the power of a centralized bureaucratic regime may be seriously impaired.[41] The third factor concerns influence. Here, problems focus on the risks to the leadership's prestige involved in pressing particular policies. Loss of influence may result in loss of support, and hence in a loss of power "income."

As Eisenstadt has shown, all three of these factors have been involved in the breakdown of higher-order political structures into some kind of feudalism. As a result, a generalized loyalty on the part of groups on whose support a regime depends—such as landowners, military officers, or civil servants—is replaced by relatively specific, more-or-less contractual relations in which loyalty is exchanged for specific perquisites and privileges. This is political barter. It is, however, noteworthy that the process of devolution usually continues further, because there is a strong tendency for the control of such resources to become hereditary and traditionalized. Hence, the devolution from generalized support to barter often proceeds to ascription of rights to resources and support. Broadly speaking, this is what happened in the breakdown of the political authority of the Roman Empire.

Thus, we may regard a polity as maintaining its power potential through continual interchanges with its environment. On the one hand, it "exports" power in the form of opportunity for effectiveness, and gets in return power in the form of commitment of services. On the other hand, it "exports" power in the form of policy decisions, and gets in return power in the form of political support.

Such interchanges function to ensure that needs for financial resources or influence will not drain the polity's allocable power potential more rapidly than they can be balanced by inputs into the polity. These considerations should make clear the vital importance of the *generalization* as media of both power and influence as well as of money. Without such generalized media, it is impossible to transcend the level of differentiation which uses what I have called *political barter*. Such barter, however, seems to be in-

[41] S. N. Eisenstadt, *The Political Systems of Empires* (New York: Free Press of Glencoe, Inc., 1963), esp. pp. 342 ff.

herently unstable: without adequate generalization of both power and influence, ascriptive rigidity is almost inevitable.

In economic structures, a positive balance of the medium is maintained by regulating action with the standard of solvency—the requirement that monetary income balance monetary expenditures in market transactions. Units having political primacy, which must balance power outputs with power inputs, are governed by a parallel standard. With some trepidation, I will appropriate the old term *sovereignty* for this standard, though in a very non-Austinian sense. I mean to emphasize its implication of political independence, but in a sense applying to both governmental and private collectivities. Contrary to the Austinian conception, I assume a normative order superordinate to the "sovereignty" of any unit within a social system, including a national government. In these terms, a business firm is sovereign insofar as it maintains the authority of its offices and attracts both services and support without depending upon political subsidy, or the use of another collectivity's factors of effectiveness. Along with solvency, this is clearly the ideal of free enterprise.[42] Regarding territorial governments, the acceptance of a controlling normative order need not imply an impairment of sovereignty.

Units failing to maintain sovereignty must obtain inputs of power in addition to the "proceeds" of their own operations, or they must forego some of their capacity to command binding political obligations. This impairment of sovereignty regularly occurs in declining political systems, such as the declining empires Eisenstadt analyzes,[43] which disintegrate into components and/or become absorbed in other polities. Parallel considerations apply to various types of private collectivities, such as business firms and political parties.

Growth

The modes of losing strict sovereignty include, however, a special case connected with problems of growth. A collectivity may become committed to the ambition to expand the system's power capacity to a degree which cannot be fulfilled by internal resources. It must then obtain an additional input of power which need not be immediately balanced by an output; in other words, power must be "borrowed." This is a political parallel to the extension of credit to an economic unit, which may then increase its productivity by proper investment, and eventually repay the loan, with interest, on terms compatible with its long-run solvency.

This raises the question of whether political power is subject to zero-

---

[42] See S. M. Lipset: *The First New Nation* (New York: Free Press of Glencoe, Inc., 1963), for evidence that American businesses, however, have often been amenable to accepting political subsidy from government under certain circumstances.

[43] Eisenstadt, *Political Systems of Empires.*

sum conditions, as a majority of authorities on the subject seem to hold.[44] I suggest that political systems have mechanisms which are strictly parallel to credit-creation through banking, and which can also make net additions to the circulating medium. These mechanisms operate through a particular mode of relation between power and influence and involve the agencies using these media.

The generalization of political support, which precludes its being conditioned to particular policy decisions in *quid-pro-quo* fashion, is comparable to the deposit of money in a bank. Although elected leaders are, to be sure, responsible for safeguarding their constituents' interests, they are not obligated to use power only with specific authorization from their constituencies. Insofar as they make policy decisions without such particular authorization, they may bind the collectivity to commitments which can be jeopardized by a mass withdrawal of political support. Voters are no more obligated to re-elect leaders who have made commitments of which they disapprove than depositors are obligated to keep funds in a bank that makes loans which they believe to be economically unsound. It is, however, precisely through the lending of funds which depositors have a right to withdraw on demand that banks can make a net addition to the circulating medium through the *creation* of credit. Similarly, political leadership can make a net addition to the power in the system by taking responsibility for decisions which are not specifically authorized by the constituency. One consequence, however, is that a functioning political leadership, like a bank management, is always unable to meet all its formal obligations instantaneously; in this sense, the bank is insolvent, and the polity fails to guarantee its sovereignty.

Bank loans increase the amount of money in circulation by using power in the form of binding contractual commitments. The banker not only requires his borrowers to repay their loans at stated times, but he himself is bound not to demand early repayments even though his depositors may demand repayment of their funds at *any* time. Thus the banker takes the risk that a loss of confidence in the bank may touch off a run by depositors, catching him unable to pay. In monetary systems, of course, power is also explicitly used when the power of the government is put behind the stability of the banking system through, for example, a central banking system which is ultimately controlled by the government. Such added security may be an essential condition of a bank's capacity to expand credit without making the depositors' positions unduly insecure. Similarly, a political leader cannot guarantee that policy commitments obligating the collectivity

---

[44] Lasswell and Kaplan, *Power and Society;* C. W. Mills, *The Power Elite* (New York: Oxford University Press, 1956); Key, *Politics, Parties, and Pressure Groups;* R. A. Dahl, "The Concept of Power," *Behavioral Science,* II (1957) 201–15); and Dahl, *Modern Political Analysis,* Chapter Five.

for longer than his own term of office will be honored—the voters may throw him out in favor of a candidate pledged to repudiate his policy commitments. Yet, he "uses his influence" both to persuade those affected, whether inside or outside his collectivity, to regard such commitments as genuine and to persuade his electorate to support them. For example, the federal government carries long-term obligations to finance scientific research and development even though Congress may legally terminate the whole program at nearly any time by refusing to appropriate the requisite funds.

The successful extention of binding commitments not specifically authorized by the supporting constituencies can provide *net* additions to the power potential of the polity as a whole by making binding decisions stick despite costs in resources and leadership prestige. This comprises "prudent investment" in the increase of power if the conditions of long-run growth are met, so that the system's potential increases by degrees commensurate with the increase of commitments enforceable with power.

Detailed analyses of such processes are confronted by many complications. There is no space here to present even a few examples. I hope, however, that I have created sufficient presumption in favor of the two following propositions so that, when they are specified empirically, they will not simply be dismissed as absurd.

First, power is not a zero-sum resource: an increase in the amount of power held by one unit in a system does not necessarily involve a corresponding diminution in the power held by the other units in the same system. The crucial analogy is that, in accepting a bank loan, a unit does not normally diminish the money available to the bank's depositors. Similarly, the voters' power to select leadership is not impaired by the normal promulgation of commitments by their leaders.

An important difference between the two cases, however, affects the definition of conditions under which increments to the media are possible. Loans are pie slices which may vary in size on a continuous scale. But policy decisions are all-or-none commitments, competing with alternative commitments, which either prevail or fail, in many cases without possibility of compromise. This difference does not, however, invalidate the applicability of the general model of net increase through positive commitment despite risk factors.

Second, the leverage for increase in a given medium must come from the next-higher subsystem in the hierarchy of control. Credit creation is not possible through monetary manipulation alone—it requires the mobilization of power in the form of binding contractual obligations. Similarly, power cannot be increased simply by internal manipulation of power relations in the political system. It requires the mobilization of influence, the use of which must be justified in terms of institutionalized norms. For specific agents, this means laying prestige and future potential for influence on the line in favor of the policy to which they wish to give the bindingness of power.[45]

Growth in a political system, as measured by changes in its power potential, may arise from exogenous sources, such as economic growth independent of political changes or improvements in the environment of the society. The growth process just outlined, however, is primarily endogenous. It requires articulation with the influence system, which is not, analytically, in the polity, although it can be oriented mainly to the polity or to relevant sectors of the polity.

Structural change

The third type of process to be discussed is institutional change in the structural components of the polity.[46] Here I will treat the problems of analyzing changes that contribute to evolutionary advancement, since I have remarked on devolutionary processes above. Modern examples are the development of the democratic franchise, as traced by Rokkan and his associates, or, in the private sphere, the transformation of family-firm entrepreneurship into corporate organization which differentiates the functions of ownership from those of active management.[47] From one point of view, the key aspect of such a process of structural development is differentiation —that is, the division of one previous structure into two, as when specialized units of economic production (firms) are differentiated from family households. At least three further processes must, however, take place if the outcome of a process of differentiation is to be stabilized. First, *both* units (or classes of units) must be included in a new level of collective organization—in this case, in a new type of local community which includes both units of residence and of employment. Second, norms must be generalized to the point where they can regulate action in both types of unit and the relations between them. Thus, property relations can no longer be regulated on the assumption that only households can hold property rights.

---

[45] This does not imply that concrete organizations cannot autonomously generate increases in their media. Firms ploughing back their profits into investment fuse the productive and banking functions in one concrete organization. Similarly a party in office may use both power and influence to invest in the increase of power.

[46] See Parsons and Smelser, *Economy and Society;* Talcott Parsons, "Some Considerations on the Theory of Social Change," *Rural Sociology,* XXVI (September, 1961), 217–39, for general discussions of problems in analyzing institutional change.

[47] Smelser and I used this example, roughly analyzed, to illustrate our paradigm of social change in *Economy and Society,* Chapter Five. The classical description and discussion of this example is in A. A. Berle and G. C. Means, *The Modern Corporation and Private Property* (New York: Commerce Clearing House, Inc., 1932). An excellent current example is the process leading toward full inclusion of the Negro in the American polity with full rights of participation and equal opportunity. For a particularly pertinent study of this process, see Leon Mayhew, "Law and Equal Opportunity: Anti-Discrimination Law in Massachusetts" (Doctoral dissertation, Harvard University, 1964).

Third, there must be an up-grading of the processes by which resources are made available to the newly differentiated operative units, so that their stricter exigencies can be met.

In such cases, not only must a need for the relevant change develop, but also any previously institutionalized norms which conflict with the newly emerging structure must be questioned. To legitimize a change of norms, it is necessary both to alter the constellation of interests and to invoke the value-system itself at requisite levels of specificity on behalf of the new norms. In the American race problem, this has been done by judicial declarations that the "separate but equal" doctrine is incompatible with the basic value-principle of "equal protection of the laws."

Legitimation of a change in norms, however, is not sufficient. It is necessary to deal with what Leon Mayhew, in the case of the race issue, calls "structural discrimination." Modes of action previously treated as acceptable and at least partially legitimate have to be coped with and changed. Examples are beliefs that only the community's "responsible" elements should be entrusted with the franchise, that the "impersonality" of corporate firms has destroyed the "paternalistic intimacy" of family firms having tangible, responsible bosses, and that people's rights to choose their own neighbors are violated by antidiscriminatory housing legislation.

Precisely because any normative system allows for alternative interpretations, the bearing that the new norms have on accepted values must be clarified. Concurrently, the definition of the situation with respect to practical interests must change enough so that an adequately large and strategically placed group develops an interest in actuating the new norms.

These three types of process involve a progressively widening circle of factors in the operation of a given political system. Circular-flow processes can be viewed as entirely intrapolitical in their processual mechanisms, though they involve responses to changes in the situation of the polity. Political growth, even when mainly endogenous, involves a specific mode of articulation with the next higher system in the hierarchy of control, which I call *the integrative system,* for which influence is the generalized medium. This mode is the mobilization of influence, a medium which is not (like power) primarily political, to increase the effectiveness of a political unit by "investing" in the increase of its power. Processes of change in the institutional structure of a political system require a still more complex process. They involve influence even more crucially because it must be used more broadly and must be backed by explicit references to generalized value-commitments in order to legitimize the changed norms that justify the given exercises of influence.

CONCLUSION

The above is a very sketchy, abstract outline of an approach to the analysis of what I deliberately call the political *aspect* of a society or other social system. I use this term to emphasize that the political system, or polity, is analytically defined and, hence, is an abstracted subsystem of a total social system which must systematically articulate with the other subsystems—the economy, the integrative system, and the pattern-maintenance system—abstracted at a comparable level.

While attempting to account for the many crucial substantive differences between polity and economy, I have tried throughout to follow the mode of analysis which Smelser and myself used to analyze the economy and its place in the society. Perhaps the main point of my analysis is the conception of political power as a generalized medium of political process that parallels the role of money in economic process.

Also paralleling the economic paradigm, I have stressed that the polity is not a closed system, but is engaged in continual interchanges with adjacent systems, the economic and the integrative. This crucial proposition seems to imply the disproof of two very important trends in recent literature on power. First is the idea that power is inherently hierarchical and necessarily dissociated from any egalitarian elements in social systems. Contrary to this, I have contended that equality of the franchise and the regulation of commitment to service by the equality-of-opportunity principle are authentic modes of institutionalizing power systems in relation to the boundary exigencies of the polity. Second is the assumption that zero-sum conditions always apply to power circulation. I have challenged this with the conception that influence may be used in certain circumstances to increase the power potential of a political system.

In this connection, a series of problems concerning the structure of political systems were discussed, notably in the fields of bureaucratic organization and democratic association, the latter with special regard to electoral systems. Then three types of process in political systems were sketchily outlined, with Schumpeter's analysis of economic process providing a principal model. These processes of circular flow, growth, and structural change were arranged according to the increasing factors exogenous to the polity which they involve and according to the complexity of the modes of such involvement which they require.

Whatever its limitations, I believe this to be a valuable approach to the systematic theoretical treatment of political systems. Though not developed very far, it is relatively systematic itself and relates systematically to both the conception of a society as a whole and the conception of a social system as part of a more general action system. These two latter points, indeed, I consider to be among its most important virtues.

APPENDIX: TECHNICAL NOTE

This short appendix cannot explain the Theory of Action, even in its simplest form. Its major purpose is to indicate some of the bases of the claim made in the body of the paper that the present analysis of political structures genuinely derives from a general theory. Readers already somewhat familiar with the theory, however, should find the formal paradigms presented below helpful for understanding the technical interrelations of the categories used above and of those applying to other aspects of social systems and the other action systems. For readers unfamiliar with the Theory of Action, these notes briefly outline certain of the basic, general conceptions from which much of the foregoing analysis derives.[48]

Perhaps the fundamental assumption of the theory is that, within the action frame of reference which focuses on the decision making that patterns action, all acts necessarily have *meaning* relative to the conditions of action situations and, through that meaning, systematic relations to one another. Therefore, the theory is based upon a general conception of system that has been developed to apply specifically to the conditions and characteristics of action. On formal grounds, the four-function paradigm, which orders concepts throughout the theory, derives directly from this idea of a boundary-maintaining system. Our present concern is with the use of the scheme to analyze *social* systems.

Pattern maintenance involves upholding the basic ordering principles of the system with regard to both the value of such patterns and the commitment of system units to them. Integration concerns the adjustment of relations among the units of a system, particularly with regard to the allocation of advantages and disadvantages, to ensure that the units will contribute to an order desirable for the system. Goal attainment consists of coordinated actions taken by plural units collectively to bring about valued relations between the system and its environment, particularly insofar as prior to action such relations fail to meet requirements of the system. Adaptation involves the development of disposable resources useful for wide varieties of specific purposes to increase the system's capacity to cope with its environment under varying conditions. Any system must function adequately in each of these respects if it is to continue operations over time. Taken in the order presented, the four functions prescribe a cybernetic

---

[48] For a more extensive treatment of the theory, see Talcott Parsons, "An Outline of the Social System," in *Theories of Society,* eds. Talcott Parsons, Edward Shils, K. D. Naegele, and J. R. Pitts (New York: Free Press of Glencoe, Inc., 1961), Vol. I, pp. 30–79. Two of my articles previously cited, "On the Concept of Political Power" and "On the Concept of Influence," are my most general treatments of the media in the context of interchange processes. My "Evolutionary Universals in Society," *American Sociological Review,* XXIX (June, 1964), 339–57; and my *Societies: Comparative and Evolutionary Perspectives* treat the problem of social evolution. Smelser, *Theory of Collective Behavior* (New York: Free Press of Glencoe, Inc., 1963), and Parsons and Smelser, *Economy and Society* contain much material on social processes, particularly on the concept of interchanges. Talcott Parsons and Edward Shils, "Values, Motives, and Systems of Action," in *Toward a General Theory of Action,* eds. Talcott Parsons and Edward Shils (Cambridge: Harvard University Press, 1951), is an early and basic treatment of the theory.

hierarchy of control over conditions—determination in regard to higher functions orders action emerging at lower levels, but only within the spheres of conditions that are, in turn, ordered at the lower levels. Because, in the first instance, these categories are purely definitional, they may be applied to all types of action systems. And, although the full reasons cannot be presented here, they may be regarded as theoretically exhaustive for any action system of reference when used at the proper level of generality; all relevant empirical information can be ordered within them and within their interrelationships.

Because the four functions denote distinct exigencies which action systems must meet, the systems may be conceived of as tending to develop specialized means for performing each function. In the case of relatively complex systems, such specialization may be regarded as taking the form of differentiated subsystems. Thus, at the most general level, cultural, social, personality, and behavioral-organism subsystems perform respectively the pattern-maintenance, integrative, goal-attainment, and adaptive functions for the action system. These systems are to be seen not as statically distinct, but as having dynamic interrelations like those of the societal subsystems discussed below. Above all, it must be kept in mind that distinctions between subsystems are highly analytic and well-removed from the concrete. Moreover, this fact does not become less important as the theory is specified to more detailed, concrete structures.

Here I can treat only the social subsystem of action and, within that category, only highly developed whole societies. Pattern-maintenance is performed primarily by religious groups concerned with developing the pattern of the general values of the society, and by nuclear families which socialize their members, upholding their commitments to social values. However, a variety of other structures, particularly schools and universities, are also involved in pattern-maintenance. The integrative subsystem is concerned with the problems of stratification and social control in their relations to institutionalized communities and their constitutive social norms. Under the control of the norms, the numerous, crosscutting segments of the society must be included in, and loyal to, a solidary *societal* community, and the terms of societal membership with regard to rights and obligations must permit adequate associational mobilization and articulation of legitimate interests and commitments. The goal-attainment subsystem is the polity, consisting of collectivities, governmental and private, which contribute organizational capacities to the achievement of the goals of the society and its subsystems. The adaptive subsystem is the economy, conceived of as the system within which the classical economic factors are mobilized, combined in the processes of production, and made available to public or private consumers. Each of these four functionally defined subsystems may in turn be analyzed into component subsystems, as has been done for the polity in the body of the paper.

Fundamentally, there are two structural reference points for analyzing

The investment process, which I conceive of as an important special case of the operation of this interchange system, seems to work so that the power component of a loan is a grant of opportunity through which an otherwise unavailable increment in control of productivity may be gained. The recipient of this grant, through committing individual or collective services, is placed in a position to utilize these resources for increasing economic productivity. This is a special case because the resource might be used in some other way, e.g., for relieving distress or for scientific research.

In the G-I (polity-integrative system) interchange, power is inter-

Figure 2. The Categories of Societal Interchange.

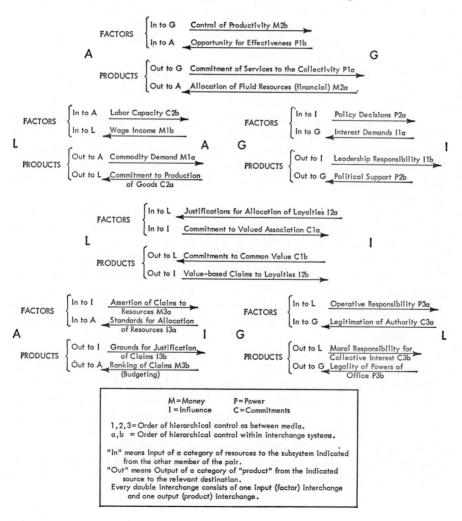

changed not with money, but with influence. Whereas, vis-à-vis money, power is the "controlling" medium in the cybernetic hierarchy, vis-à-vis influence, power itself is "controlled." This difference is symbolized in the paradigm by placing the power categories in the outside positions in the G-I interchange, while in the A-G case they are placed inside (as the monetary categories were in L-A).

Here the factor interchange is between policy decisions as a "factor of solidarity" and interest demands as a "factor of effectiveness." Essentially, we may say that interest demands "define the situation" for political decision making—which is by no means to say that demands in their initial form are or should be simply granted without modification. Like other factors, they are typically transformed in the course of political process. Correspondingly, policy decisions are a factor in solidarity because, properly framed, they reliably obligate the collectivity to attain goals in which interested parties of various sorts have justifiable stakes, grounded in the rights and privileges of community membership.

As a "product" output, leadership responsibility (a form of influence, not of power) as an output of the polity is exchanged for political support as an output of an "associational" system, e.g., a political party which mobilizes the political "income" of power in the governmental case. It should be noted that the units involved in any particular case of these two interchanges are typically not the same. Thus, party leaders may bid for support, whereas administrative officials may make salient decisions. This type of split (carried out to varying degrees) is a necessary characteristic of any highly differentiated system.

Figure 3 views the generalized media in terms not only of their hierarchical ordering, but also of the relation between their code and message components, including the sanction aspects of the message components which control both factors essential to the various functional subsystems and "product" outputs from these subsystems. The rows, each of which designates one of the four media, are arranged from top to bottom in terms of the hierarchy of control. The columns designate some elements into which each medium must be analyzed if the basic conditions of its operation in mediating interaction are to be understood.

Informally, the body of the paper made clear some reasons for distinguishing two components in the code aspects of each medium; its value-principle and its coordinative standard. The most familiar example is the paradigmatic economic case. Here, the famous concept of *utility* seems to be relevant as the value-principle, while solvency may serve as the coordinative standard. Utility is the basic measure of value in the economic sense, whereas the imperative of maintaining solvency is an important norm guiding units in economic action. I have adopted Barnard's concept of *effectiveness* as the political parallel to utility. Sovereignty for the relevant

COMPONENTS OF MEDIA AND INTERCHANGE RECIPROCALS / MEDIA IN HIERARCHY OF CONTROL	CODES		MESSAGES (SANCTIONS)		TYPES OF SANCTION AND OF EFFECT
	VALUE-PRINCIPLE	COORDINATION STANDARD	FACTORS CONTROLLED	PRODUCTS CONTROLLED	
			SOURCE	DESTINATION	
L COMMITMENTS	INTEGRITY	PATTERN CONSISTENCY	WAGES A JUSTIFICATION OF LOYALTIES I	CONSUMER'S DEMAND A CLAIMS TO LOYALTIES I	NEGATIVE-INTENTIONAL (ACTIVATION OF COMMITMENTS)
I INFLUENCE	SOLIDARITY	CONSENSUS	COMMITMENTS TO VALUED ASSOCIATION L POLICY DECISIONS G	COMMITMENT TO COMMON VALUES L POLITICAL SUPPORT G	POSITIVE-INTENTIONAL (PERSUASION)
G POWER	EFFECTIVENESS	SOVEREIGNTY	INTEREST DEMANDS I CONTROL OF PRODUCTIVITY A	LEADERSHIP RESPONSIBILITY I CONTROL OF FLUID RESOURCES A	NEGATIVE-SITUATIONAL (SECURING COMPLIANCE)
A MONEY	UTILITY	SOLVENCY	CAPITAL G LABOR L	COMMITMENT OF SERVICES G EXPECTATION OF GOODS L	POSITIVE-SITUATIONAL (INDUCEMENT)

Figure 3. The Media as Sanctions.

collectivity seems to be the best term for the political coordinative standard, if it is used with proper qualification.

Solidarity in Durkheim's sense seems to be the value-principle of integration, parallel to economic utility and political effectiveness. The concept of *consensus*, so important to political theory, seems to formulate adequately the integrative coordinative standard. In the pattern-maintenance system, the value-principle seems to be integrity and the coordinative standard seems to be pattern consistency.

The A and G columns of Figure 3 designate contexts of operation of each of the four media as sanctions, arranged by control of factor inputs and "product" outputs respectively, rather than by interchange system as in Figure 2. Thus money, though not itself a factor of production, "controls"— that is, buys—labor (in A-L) and capital (in A-G) as the primary factors. For "consuming" systems, on the other hand, money buys outputs of the economy, namely goods (in A-L) and services (in A-G).

The involvement of power is conceived to be parallel. First, it commands the two primary mobile factors of effectiveness, control of productivity (in G-A) and interest demands (in G-I), as justified in terms of appeal to norms. Second, the consumers or beneficiaries of the outputs of political process can use power to command these outputs in the form of fluid resources, e.g., through budget allocation (in G-A), and leadership responsibility for valued goals (in G-I).

Returning to Figure 2, power as code is involved in the legitimation system as an aspect of authority. This may be conceived of as a mechanism for linking the principles and standards in the L and G rows of Figure 3. Operative responsibility (P3a in Figure 2), which is treated as a factor of integrity, is responsibility for sovereign implementation of the value-principles, and involves not only collective effectiveness, but also integrity to the paramount societal value-pattern. One can say that the legitimation of authority "imposes" the responsibility to maintain such sovereignty. Legality of the powers of office (P3c in Figure 2), however, as a category of output to the polity, is an application of the standard of pattern consistency. At the various relevant levels, action may and should be taken consistently with the value-commitments. In exchange for legal authorization to take such action, the responsible office-holder must accept moral responsibility for his use of power and his interpretive decisions.

FIVE

M. G. SMITH

University of California, Los Angeles

A Structural Approach
to Comparative Politics

Comparative politics seeks to discover regularities and variations of political organization by comparative analysis of historical and contemporary systems. Having isolated these regularities and variations, it seeks to determine the factors which underlie them, in order to discover the properties and conditions of polities of varying types. It then seeks to reduce these observations to a series of interconnected propositions applicable to all these systems in both static and changing conditions. Hopefully, one can then enquire how these governmental processes relate to the wider milieux of which they are part.

It would seem that this comparative enquiry may be pursued in various ways that all share the same basic strategy, but differ in emphases and starting points. Their common strategy is to abstract one aspect of political reality and develop it as a frame of reference. With this variable held constant, enquiries can seek to determine the limits within which other dimensions vary; as the value of the primary variable is changed, the forms and values of the others, separately or together, can also be investigated. Ideally, we should seek to deduce relevant hypotheses from a general body of theory, and then to check and refine them by inductive analyses of historical and ethnographic data. Actual procedures vary.

Initially, we might expect any one of four approaches to be useful in the comparative study of political systems. These four approaches use respectively the dimensions of process, content, function, and form as the bases for their conceptual frameworks. In fact, comparative studies based on process and content face insuperable obstacles due to the enormous variability of political systems. In centralized polities, the institutional processes of government are elaborately differentiated, discrete, and easy to identify. They are often the subject, as well as the source, of a more or less complex and precise body of rules which may require specialists to interpret them. In simpler societies, the corresponding processes are rarely differentiated and discrete. They normally occur within the context of institutional activities with multiple functions, and are often difficult to abstract and segregate for analysis as self-contained processual systems. Before this is possible, we need independent criteria to distinguish the governmental and nongovernmental dimensions of these institutional forms.

The substantive approach rests on the category of content. By the content of a governmental system, I mean its specific substantive concerns and resources, whether material, human, or symbolic. As a rule, the more differentiated and complex the governmental processes are, the greater the range and complexity of content. This follows because the content and processes of government vary together. Since both these frameworks are interdependent and derivative, both presuppose independent criteria for identifying government.

The functional approach avoids these limitations. It defines government functionally as all those activities which influence "the way in which authoritative decisions are formulated and executed for a society."[1] From this starting point, various refined conceptual schemes can be developed. As requisites or implications of these decisional processes, David Easton identifies five modes of action as necessary elements of all political systems: legislation, administration, adjudication, the development of demands, and the development of support and solidarity. They may be grouped as input and output requisites of governmental systems. According to Almond, the universally necessary inputs are political socialization and recruitment, interest articulation, interest aggregation, and political communication. As outputs, he states that rule making, rule application, and rule adjudication are all universal.[2] Neither of these categorical schemes specifies foreign relations and defense, which are two very general governmental concerns; nor is it easy to see how these schemes could accommodate political processes in non-societal units.

Such deductive models suffer from certain inexplicit assumptions with-

[1] David Easton, "An Approach to the Analysis of Political Systems," *World Politics,* IX, No. 3 (1957), 384.
[2] Gabriel Almond, "Introduction" to Almond and James S. Coleman, *The Politics of the Developing Areas* (Princeton: Princeton University Press, 1961).

out which the initial exclusive stress on political functions might be impossible. But despite their universal claims, it remains to be shown that Bushmen, Pygmies, or Eskimos have governments which are functionally homologous with those of the United States and the Soviet Union. Legislation, rule adjudication, and interest articulation are categories appropriate to the discussion of complex, modern polities rather than simple, primitive ones. But the problem which faces the student of comparative politics is to develop a conceptual framework useful and applicable to all. To impute the features and conditions of modern polities to the less differentiated primitive systems is virtually to abandon the central problem of comparative politics.

The functional approach, as usually presented, suffers from a further defect: It assumes a rather special ensemble of structural conditions. When "authoritative decisions are formulated and executed for a society," this unit must be territorially delimited and politically centralized. The mode of centralization should also endow government with "more-or-less legitimate physical compulsion."[3] In short, the reality to which the model refers is the modern nation-state.

By such criteria, ethnography shows that the boundaries of many societies are fluctuating and obscure, and that the authoritative status of decisions made in and for them are even more so. Clearly bounded societies with centralized authority systems are perhaps a small minority of the polities with which we have to deal. A structural approach free of these functional presumptions may thus be useful, but only if it can accommodate the full range of political systems and elucidate the principles which underlie their variety. In this paper, I shall only indicate the broad outlines of this approach. I hope to present it more fully in the future.

Government is the regulation of public affairs. This regulation is a set of processes which defines government functionally, and which also identifies its content as the affairs which are regulated, and the resources used to regulate them. It does not seem useful or necessary to begin a comparative study of governmental systems by deductive theories which predicate their minimum universal content, requisites, or features. The critical element in government is its public character. Without a public, there can be neither public affairs nor processes to regulate them. Moreover, while all governments presuppose publics, all publics have governments for the management of their affairs. The nature of these publics is therefore the first object of study.

Publics vary in scale, composition, and character, and it is reasonable to suppose that their common affairs and regulatory arrangements will vary correspondingly. The first task of a structural approach to comparative politics is thus to identify the properties of a public and to indicate the principal varieties and bases of publics.

[3] Almond, "Introduction," p. 7.

As I use the term, *public* does not include mobs, crowds, casual assemblies, or mass-communication audiences. It does not refer to such categories as resident aliens, the ill, aged, or unwed, or to those social segments which lack common affairs and organized procedures to regulate them—for example, slaves, some clans, and unenfranchised strata such as the medieval serfs or the *harijans* of India. Such categories are part of one or more publics; they are not separate publics of their own. For example, in an Indian village, a medieval manor, or a slave plantation, members of the disprivileged categories constitute a public only if they form an enduring group having certain common affairs and the organization and autonomy necessary to regulate them; but the existence of such local publics is not in itself sufficient for the strata from which their memberships are drawn to have the status of publics. For this to be the case, these local publics must be organized into a single group co-extensive with the stratum. With such organization, we shall expect to find a set of common affairs and procedures to regulate them. The organization is itself an important common affair and a system of institutional procedures.

By a *public,* then, I mean an enduring, presumably perpetual group with determinate boundaries and membership, having an internal organization and a unitary set of external relations, an exclusive body of common affairs, and autonomy and procedures adequate to regulate them.

It will be evident that a public can neither come into being nor maintain its existence without some set of procedures by which it regulates its internal and external affairs. These procedures together form the governmental process of the public. Mobs, crowds, and audiences are not publics, because they lack presumptive continuity, internal organization, common affairs, procedures, and autonomy. For this reason, they also lack the determinate boundaries and membership which are essential for a durable group. While the categories mentioned above are fixed and durable, they also lack the internal organization and procedures which constitute a group.

When groups are constituted so that their continuity, identity, autonomy, organization, and exclusive affairs are not disturbed by the entrance or exit of their individual members, they have the character of a public. The city of Santa Monica shares these properties with the United States, the Roman Catholic Church, Bushman bands, the dominant caste of an Indian village, the Mende *Poro,* an African lineage, a Nahuatl or Slavonic village community, Galla and Kikuyu age-sets, societies among the Crow and Hidatsa Indians, universities, medieval guilds, chartered companies, regiments,. and such "voluntary" associations as the Yoruba *Ogboni,* the Yako *Ikpungkara,* and the American Medical Association. The units just listed are all publics and all are corporate groups; the governmental process inherent in publics is a feature of all corporate groups.

Corporate groups—Maine's "corporations aggregate"—are one species of "perfect" or fully-fledged corporation, the other being the "corporation sole" exemplified by such offices as the American Presidency, the British Crown, the Papacy, governorships, chieftaincies, and university chancellorships. Corporations sole and corporate groups share the following characteristics, all of which are necessary for "perfect" or full corporate status: identity, presumed perpetuity, closure and membership, autonomy within a given sphere, exclusive common affairs, set procedures, and organization. The first four of these qualities are formal and primarily external in their reference; they define the unit in relation to its context. The last four conditions are processual and functional, and primarily internal in their reference.

The main differences between corporations sole and corporate groups are structural, though developmental differences are also important. Corporate groups are pluralities to which an unchanging unity is ascribed; viewed externally, each forms *"one person,"* as Fortes characterized the Ashanti matrilineages.[4] This external indivisibility of the corporate group is not merely a jural postulate. It inevitably presumes and involves governmental processes within the group.

In contrast with a corporate group, an office is a unique status having only one incumbent at any given time. Nonetheless, successive holders of a common office are often conceived of and addressed as a group. The present incumbent is merely one link in a chain of indefinite extent, the temporary custodian of all the properties, powers, and privileges which constitute the office. As such, incumbents may legitimately seek to aggrandize their offices at the expense of similar units or of the publics to which these offices relate; but they are not personally authorized to alienate or reduce the rights and powers of the status temporarily entrusted to them. The distinction between the capital of an enterprise and the personalty of its owners is similar to the distinction between the office and its incumbent. It is this distinction that enables us to distinguish offices from other personal statuses most easily.

It is very possible that in social evolution the corporate group preceded the corporation sole. However, once authority is adequately centralized, offices tend to become dominant; and then we often find that offices are instituted in advance of the publics they will regulate or represent, as, for example, when autocrats order the establishment of new towns, settlements, or colonies under officials designated to set up and administer them. There are many instances in which corporate groups and offices emerge and develop in harmony and congruence, and both may often lapse at once as, for example, when a given public is conquered and assimilated.

These developmental relations are merely one aspect of the very variable but fundamental relation between offices and corporate groups. Despite Weber, there are a wide range of corporate groups which lack stable leaders,

---

[4] Meyer Fortes, "Kinship and Marriage among the Ashanti," in *African Systems of Kinship and Marriage,* eds. A. R. Radcliffe-Brown and Daryll Forde (London: Oxford University Press, 1950), pp. 254–61.

much less official heads. Others may have senior members whose authority is at best advisory and representative; yet others have a definite council or an official head, or both. In many cases, we have to deal with a public constituted by a number of coordinate corporate groups of similar type. The senior members of these groups may form a collegial body to administer the common affairs of the public, with variable powers. Ibo and Indian village communities illustrate this well. In such contexts, where superordinate offices emerge, they often have a primarily sacred symbolic quality, as do the divine kingships of the Ngonde and Shilluk, but lack effective secular control. Between this extreme and an absolute despotism, there are a number of differing arrangements which only a comparative structural analysis may reduce to a single general order.

Different writers stress different features of corporate organization, and sometimes employ these to "explain" these social forms. Weber, who recognizes the central role of corporate groups in political systems, fails to distinguish them adequately from offices (or "administrative organs," as he calls them).[5] For Weber, corporate groups are defined by coordinated action under leaders who exercise de facto powers of command over them. The inadequacy of this view is patent when Barth employs it as the basis for denying to lineages and certain other units the corporate status they normally have, while reserving the term corporate for factions of a heterogeneous and contingent character.[6] Maine, on the other hand, stresses the perpetuity of the corporation and its inalienable bundle of rights and obligations, the estate with which it is indentified.[7] For Gierke,[8] Durkheim,[9] and Davis,[10] corporate groups are identified by their common will, collective conscience, and group personality. For Goody, only named groups holding material property in common are corporate.[11]

These definitions all suffer from overemphasis on some elements, and corresponding inattention to others. The common action characteristic of corporate groups rarely embraces the application of violence which both Weber and Barth seem to stress. Mass violence often proceeds independ-

[5] Max Weber, The Theory of Social and Economic Organization, trans. A. R. Henderson and Talcott Parsons (London: Wm. Hodge & Co., 1947), pp. 133–37, 302–5.

[6] Fredrik Barth, Political Leadership among Swat Pathans. Monographs in Social Anthropology, London School of Economics, No. 19 (London: University of London Press, 1959).

[7] H. S. Maine, Ancient Law (London: Routledge & Kegan Paul, Ltd., 1904), p. 155.

[8] Otto Gierke, Natural Law and the Theory of Society, 1500 to 1800, trans. Ernest Barker (Boston: Beacon Press, 1957).

[9] Emile Durkheim, The Division of Labour in Society, trans. George E. Simpson (New York: Free Press of Glencoe, Inc., 1933).

[10] John P. Davis, Corporations (New York: Capricorn Books, 1961), p. 34.

[11] Jack Goody, "The Classification of Double Descent Systems," Current Anthropology, II, No. 1 (1961), 5, 22–3.

ently of corporate groups. Corporate action is typically action to regulate corporate affairs—that is, to exercise and protect corporate rights, to enforce corporate obligations, and to allocate corporate responsibilities and privileges. When a group holds a common estate, this tenure and its exercise inevitably involve corporate action, as does any ritual in which the members or representatives of the group engage as a unit. Even the maintenance of the group's identity and closure entails modes of corporate action, the complexity and implications of which vary with the situation. It is thus quite fallacious to identify corporate action solely with coordinated physical movements. A chorus is not a corporate group.

The presumed perpetuity, boundedness, determinate membership, and identity of a corporation, all more or less clearly entail one another, as do its requisite features of autonomy, organization, procedure, and common affairs. It is largely because of this interdependence and circularity among their elements that corporations die so hard; but by the same token, none of these elements alone can constitute or maintain a corporation.

An office persists as a unit even if it is not occupied, providing that the corpus of rights, responsibilities, and powers which constitute it still persists. To modify or eliminate the office, it is necessary to modify or eliminate its content. Among !Kung bushmen, bands persist as corporate groups even when they have no members or heads[12]; these bands are units holding an inalienable estate of water holes, *veldkos* areas, etc., and constitute the fixed points of !Kung geography and society. The Bushman's world being constituted by corporate bands, the reconstitution of these bands is unavoidable, whenever their dissolution makes this necessary.

As units which are each defined by an exclusive *universitas juris,* corporations provide the frameworks of law and authoritative regulation for the societies that they constitute. The corporate estate includes rights in the persons of its members as well as in material or incorporeal goods. In simpler societies, the bulk of substantive law consists in these systems of corporate right and obligation, and includes the conditions and correlates of membership in corporate groups of differing type. In such societies, adjectival law consists in the usual modes of corporate procedure. To a much greater extent than is commonly realized, this is also the case with modern societies.

The persistence, internal autonomy, and structural uniformity of the corporations which constitute the society ensure corresponding uniformity in its jural rules and their regular application over space and time. As modal units of social process and structure, corporations provide the framework in which the jural aspects of social relations are defined and enforced.

Tribunals are merely functionally specific corporations charged with handling issues of certain kinds. Neither tribunals nor "the systematic ap-

[12] Lorna Marshall, "!Kung Bushmen Bands," *Africa,* XXX (1960), 325–55).

plication of the force of politically organized society"[13] are necessary or sufficient for the establishment of law. The law of a primitive society consists in its traditional procedures and modes of corporate action, and is implicit in the traditional rights, obligations, and conditions of corporate membership. In such societies, units which hold the same type of corporate estate are structurally homologous, and are generally articulated in such a way that each depends on the tacit recognition or active support of its fellows to maintain and enjoy its estate. Thus, in these simpler systems, social order consists in the regulation of relations between the constitutive corporations as well as within them.

In societies which lack central political organs, societal boundaries coincide with the maximum range of an identical corporate constitution, on the articulation of which the social order depends. Though the component corporations are all discrete, they are also interdependent. But they may be linked together in a number of different ways, with consequent differences in their social systems. In some cases, functionally distinct corporations may be classified together in purely formal categories, such as moieties, clans, or castes. The Kagoro of northern Nigeria illustrate this.[14] In other cases, corporations which are formally and functionally distinct may form a wider public having certain common interests and affairs. The LoDagaba of northern Ghana and Upper Volta are an example.[15] In still other cases, corporations are linked individually to one another in a complex series of alliances and associations, with overlapping margins in such a way that they all are related, directly or indirectly, in the same network. Fortes has given us a very detailed analysis of such a system among the Tallensi.[16] However they are articulated in societies which lack central institutions, it is the extensive replication of these corporate forms which defines the unit as a separate system. Institutional uniformities, which include similarities of organization, ideology, and procedure, are quite sufficient to give these acephalous societies systemic unity, even where, as among the Kachins of Burma, competing institutional forms divide the allegiance of their members.[17]

To say that corporations provide the frameworks of primitive law, and that the tribunals of modern societies are also corporate forms, is simply to say that corporations are the central agencies for the regulation of public affairs, being themselves each a separate public or organ, administering certain affairs, and together constituting wider publics or associations of publics

[13] Roscoe Pound, *Readings on the History and System of the Common Law,* 2nd ed. (Boston: Dunster House Bookshop, 1913), p. 4.

[14] M. G. Smith, "Kagoro Political Development," *Human Organization,* XIX, No. 3 (1960), 37–49.

[15] Jack Goody, "Fields of Social Control among the LoDagaba," *Journal of the Royal Anthropological Institute,* LXXXVII, Part I (1957), 75–104.

[16] Meyer Fortes, *The Dynamics of Clanship among the Tallensi* (London: Oxford University Press, 1945).

[17] E. R. Leach, *Political Systems of Highland Burma* (London: G. Bell & Sons, Ltd., 1954).

for others. By the same token, they are the sources or frameworks of disorder. In some acephalous societies, disorder seems more or less perennial, and consists mainly in strife within and between corporations. Centralization, despite its merits, does not really exclude disorder. In concentrating authority, it simultaneously concentrates the vulnerability of the system. Accordingly, in centralized societies, serious conflicts revolve around the central regulative structures, as, for instance, in secessionist or revolutionary struggles, dynastic or religious wars, and "rituals of rebellion."[18] Such conflicts with or for central power normally affect the entire social body. In acephalous societies, on the other hand, conflicts over the regime may proceed in one region without implicating the others.[19] In both the centralized and decentralized systems, the sources and objects of conflict are generally corporate. Careful study of Barth's account of the Swat Pathans shows that this is true for them also, although the aggregates directly contraposed are factions and blocs.[20]

Societal differences in the scale, type, and degree of order and coordination, or in the frequency, occasions, and forms of social conflict are important data and problems for political science. To analyze them adequately, one must use a comparative structural approach. Briefly, recent work suggests that the quality and modes of order in any social system reflect its corporate constitution—that is, the variety of corporate types which constitute it, their distinctive bases and properties, and the way in which they are related to one another. The variability of political systems which derives from this condition is far more complex and interesting than the traditional dichotomy of centralized and noncentralized systems would suggest. I have already indicated some important typological differences within the category of acephalous societies; equally significant differences within the centralized category are familiar to all. This traditional dichotomy assumes that centralization has a relatively clear meaning, from which a single, inclusive scale may be directly derived. This assumption subsumes a range of problems which require careful study; but in any event, centralization is merely one aspect of political organization, and not necessarily the most revealing.

Given variability in the relations between corporations sole and corporate groups, and in their bases and forms, it seems more useful to distinguish systems according to their structural simplicity or complexity, by reference to the variety of corporate units of differing forms, bases, and functions which they contain, and the principles which serve to articulate them. Patently, such differences in composition imply differences in the relational networks in which these corporations articulate. Such differences in structural composition simultaneously describe the variety of political forms

[18] Max Gluckman, *Rituals of Rebellion in South East Africa* (Manchester: Manchester University Press, 1954); "Introduction" to Gluckman, *Order and Rebellion in Tribal Africa* (London: Cohen & West, 1963).
[19] Leach, *Political Systems of Highland Burma.*
[20] Barth, *Political Leadership among Swat Pathans.*

and processes, and explain differences in the scale, order, and coordination of polities. This is so because corporate organization provides the framework, content, and procedures for the regulation of public affairs. For this reason, the analysis of corporate structure should be the first task in the case study of a political system and in comparative work.

For many political scientists, the concept of sovereignty is essential as the foundation of governmental order and autonomy. In my view, this notion is best dispensed with. It is a hindrance rather than a help to analysis, an unhappy solution of a very real problem which has been poorly formulated. In a system of sovereign states, no state is sovereign. As etymology shows, the idea of sovereignty derives from the historically antecedent condition of personal dominion such as kingship, and simply generalizes the essential features of this form as an ideology appropriate to legitimate and guide other forms of centralization. The real problem with which the notion of sovereignty deals is the relation between autonomy and coordination. As the fundamental myth of the modern nation-state, the concept is undoubtedly important in the study of these states; its historical or analytical usefulness is otherwise very doubtful. It seems best to formulate the problems of simultaneous coordination and autonomy in neutral terms.

As units administering exclusive common affairs, corporations presuppose well-defined spheres and levels of autonomy, which are generally no more nor less than the affairs of these units require for their adequate regulation. Where a corporation fully subsumes all the juridical rights of its members so that their corporate identification is exclusive and lifelong, the tendencies toward autarchy are generally greatest, the stress on internal autonomy most pronounced, and relations between corporations most brittle. This seems to be the case with certain types of segmentary lineage systems, such as the Tallensi. Yet even in these conditions, and perhaps to cope with them, we usually find institutional bonds of various types such as ritual cooperation, local community, intermarriage, clanship, and kinship which serve to bind the autarchic individual units into a series of wider publics, or a set of dyadic or triadic associations, the members of which belong to several such publics simultaneously. Weber's classification of corporate groups as heteronomous or autonomous, heterocephalous or autocephalous, touches only those aspects of this problem in which he was directly interested.[21] We need also to analyze and compare differing levels, types, and degrees of autonomy and dependence in differing social spheres and situations. From comparative studies of these problems, we may hope to derive precise hypotheses about the conditions and limits of corporate autonomy and articulation in systems of differing composition and span. These hypotheses should also illuminate the conditions and limits of social disorder.

Besides the "perfect" or fully-fledged corporations, offices and corpo-

[21] Weber, *Theory of Social and Economic Organization*, pp. 135–36.

rate groups, there are "imperfect" quasicorporations with must also be studied explicitly. The two main forms here are the corporate category and the commission. A corporate category is a clearly bounded, identifiable, and permanent aggregate which differs from the corporate group in lacking exclusive common affairs, autonomy, procedures adequate for their regulation, and the internal organization which constitutes the group. Viewed externally, acephalous societies may be regarded as corporate categories in their geographical contexts, since each lacks a single inclusive frame of organization. But they are categories of a rather special type, since, as we have seen, their institutional uniformity provides an effective basis for functional unity.

In medieval Europe, serfs formed a corporate category even though on particular manors they may have formed corporate groups. Among the Turkana[22] and Karimojong[23] of East Africa, age-sets are corporate categories since they lack internal organization, exclusive affairs, distinctive procedures, and autonomy. Among the nearby Kipsigi[24] and Nandi[25] clans are categorical units. These clans have names and identifying symbols, a determinate membership recruited by agnatic descent, certain ritual and social prohibitions of which exogamy is most important, and continuity over time; but they lack internal organization, common affairs, procedures and autonomy to regulate them. Though they provide a set of categories into which all members of these societies are distributed, they never function as social groups. Not far to the south, in Ruanda, the subject Hutu caste formed a corporate category not so long ago.[26] This "caste" had a fixed membership, closure, easy identification, and formed a permanent structural unit in the Tutsi state. Hutu were excluded from the political process, as a category and almost to a man. They lacked any inclusive internal organization, exclusive affairs, autonomy, or procedures to regulate them. Under their Tutsi masters, they held the status of serfs; but when universal suffrage was recently introduced, Hutu enrolled in political parties such as the Parmehutu Aprosoma which succeeded in throwing off the Tutsi yoke and expelling the monarchy.[27] In order to become corporate groups, corporate categories need to develop an effective representative organization, such for instance as may now be emerging among American Negroes. In the American case, this corporate category is seeking to organize itself in order to remove the disprivileges which define it as a category. Some corporate

[22] Philip Gulliver, "The Turkana Age Organization," *American Anthropologist*, LX (1958), 900–922.

[23] Neville Dyson-Hudson, to author, 1963.

[24] J. G. Peristiany, *The Social Institutions of the Kipsigis* (London: Routledge & Kegan Paul, Ltd., 1939).

[25] G. W. B. Huntingford, *The Nandi of Kenya* (London: Routledge & Kegan Paul, Ltd., 1953).

[26] J. J. Maquet, *The Premise of Inequality in Ruanda* (London: Oxford University Press, 1960).

[27] Marcel d'Hertefelt, "Les Elections Communales et le Consensus Politique au Rwanda." *Zaire*, XIV, Nos. 5–6 (1960), 403–38.

categories are thus merely formal units lacking common functions; others are defined by common disabilities and burdens, though lacking common affairs. Under Islam, the *dhimmi* formed such a category; in India, so do the individual castes. The disabilities and prohibitions which define categories are not always directly political; they include exogamy and ritual taboos.

Commissions differ from offices along lines which recall the differences between corporate categories and corporate groups. Like categories, commissions fall into two main classes: one class includes *ad hoc* and normally discontinuous capacities of a vaguely defined character, having diffuse or specific objects. The other class includes continuing series of indefinite number, the units of which are all defined in such general terms as to appear structurally and functionally equivalent and interchangeable. Familiar examples of the latter class are military commissions, magistracies, professorships, and priesthoods; but the sheiks and *sa'ids* of Islam belong here also. Examples of the first class, in which the powers exercised are unique but discontinuous and ill-defined, include parliamentary commissions of enquiry or other *ad hoc* commissions, and plenipotentiaries commissioned to negotiate special arrangements. In some societies, such as the Eskimo, Bushman, and Nuer, individuals having certain gifts may exercise informal commissions which derive support and authority from public opinion. The Nuer "bull," prophet, and leopard-skin priests are examples.[28] Among the Eskimos, the shaman and the fearless hunter-warrior have similar positions.[29] The persistence of these commissions, despite turnover of personnel and their discontinuous action, is perhaps the best evidence of their importance in these social systems. For their immediate publics, such commissions personalize social values of high relevance and provide agencies for *ad hoc* regulation and guidance of action. In these humble forms, we may perceive the seeds of modern bureaucracy.

Commissions are especially important as regulatory agencies in social movements under charismatic leaders, and during periods of popular unrest. The charismatic leadership is itself merely the supreme directing commission. As occasion requires, the charismatic leader creates new commissions by delegating authority and power to chosen individuals for special tasks. The careers of Gandhi, Mohammed, Hitler, and Shehu Usumanu dan Fodio in Hausaland illustrate this pattern well. So does the organization and development of the various Melanesian "cargo cults."[30] But if the commission is to be institutionalized as a unit of permanent administration, its arbitrary

[28] E. E. Evans-Pritchard, *The Nuer* (London: Oxford University Press, 1940).

[29] Kaj Birket-Smith, *The Eskimo* (London: Meuthuen & Co., Ltd., 1960); V. Stefansson, *My Life with the Eskimo* (New York: The Crowell-Collier Publishing Co., 1962).

[30] Peter Worsley, *The Trumpet Shall Sound* (London: McGibbon & Kee, 1957).

character must be replaced by set rules, procedures, and spheres of action; this institutionalization converts the commission into an office in the same way that its organization converts the corporate category into a corporate group. Moreover, in the processes by which corporate categories organize themselves as groups, charismatic leadership and its attached commissions are the critical agencies. The current movement for civil rights among American Negroes illustrates this neatly.

Any given public may include offices, commissions, corporate categories, and corporate groups of differing bases and type. In studying governmental systems, we must therefore begin by identifying publics and analyzing their internal constitution as well as their external relationships in these terms. It is entirely a matter of convenience whether we choose to begin with the smallest units and work outwards to the limits of their relational systems, or to proceed in the opposite direction. Given equal thoroughness, the results should be the same in both cases. Any governmental unit is corporate, and any public may include, wholly or in part, a number of such corporations. These units and their interrelations together define the internal order and constitution of the public and its network of external relations. Both in the analysis of particular systems and in comparative work, we should therefore begin by determining the corporate composition of the public under study, by distinguishing its corporate groups, offices, commissions, and categories, and by defining their several properties and features.

As already mentioned, we may find, in some acephalous societies, a series of linked publics with intercalary corporations and overlapping margins. We may also find that a single corporate form, such as the Mende *Poro* or the Roman Catholic Church, cuts across a number of quite distinct and mutually independent publics. An alternative mode of integration depends on the simultaneous membership of individuals in several distinct corporations of differing constitution, interest and kind. Thus, an adult Yako[31] simultaneously belongs to a patrilineage, a matrilineage, an age-set in his ward, the ward (which is a distinct corporate group), one or more functionally specific corporate associations at the ward or village level, and the village, which is the widest public. Such patterns of overlapping and dispersed membership may characterize both individuals and corporations equally. The corporations will then participate in several discrete publics, each with its exclusive affairs, autonomy, membership, and procedures, just as the individual participates in several corporations. It is this dispersed, multiple membership which is basic to societal unity, whether or not government is centralized. Even though the inclusive public with a centralized authority system is a corporate group, and a culturally distinct population

[31]Daryll Forde, *Yako Studies* (London: Oxford University Press, 1964); Kenneth Little, *The Mende of Sierra Leone* (London: Routledge & Kegan Paul, Ltd., 1951).

without this remains a corporate category, functionally both aggregates derive their underlying unities from the same mechanism of crosscutting memberships, loyalties, and cleavages.

In the structural study of a given political system, we must therefore define its corporate constitution, determine the principles on which these corporate forms are based, and see how they articulate with one another. In comparative study, we seek to determine what differences or uniformities of political process, content, and function correspond with observable differences or uniformities of corporate composition and articulation. For this purpose, we must isolate the structural principles on which the various types of corporations are based in order to determine their requisites and implications, and to assess their congruence or discongruence.

To indicate my meaning, it is sufficient to list the various principles on which corporate groups and categories may be based. These include sex, age, locality, ethnicity, descent, common property interests, ritual and belief, occupation, and "voluntary" association for diffuse or specific pursuits. Ethnographic data show that we shall rarely find corporate groups which are based exclusively on one of these principles. As a rule, their foundations combine two, three, or more principles, with corresponding complexity and stability in their organization. Thus, lineages are recruited and defined by descent, common property interests, and generally co-residence. Besides equivalence in age, age-sets presume sameness of sex and, for effective incorporation, local co-residence. Guilds typically stressed occupation and locality; but they were also united by property interests in common market facilities. In India, caste is incorporated on the principles of descent, ritual, and occupation.

Clearly, differing combinations of these basic structural principles will give rise to corporations of differing type, complexity, and capacity; and these differences will also affect the content, functions, forms, and contextual relations of the units which incorporate them. It follows that differing combinations of these differing corporate forms underlie the observable differences of order and process in political organization. This is the broad hypothesis to which the comparative structural study of political systems leads. It is eminently suited to verification or disproof. By the same token, uniformities in corporate composition and organization between, as well as within, societies should entail virtual identities of political process, content, and form. When, to the various possible forms of corporate group differentiated by the combination of structural principles on which they are based and by the relations to their corporate contexts which these entail, we add the other alternatives of office, commission, and category, themselves variable with respect to the principles which constitute them, we simultaneously itemize the principal elements which give rise to the variety of political forms, and the principles and methods by which we can reasonably hope to reduce them to a single general order. Since corporations are essential regulatory units of variable character, their different combinations encompass the entire range of variability of political systems on the functional, processual, and substantive, as well as on the structural levels.

Within this structural framework, we may also examine the nature of the regulatory process, its constituents, modes, and objectives. The basic elements of regulation are authority and power. Though always interdependent and often combined, they should not be confused. As a regulatory capacity, authority is legitimated and identified by the rules, traditions, and precedents which embody it and which govern its exercise and objects. Power is also regulatory, but is neither fully prescribed nor governed by norms and rules. Whereas authority presumes and expresses normative consensus, power is most evident in conflict and contraposition where dissensus obtains. In systems of public regulation, these conditions of consent and dissent inevitably concur, although they vary in their forms, objects, and proportions. Such systems accordingly depend on the simultaneous exercise and interrelation of the power and authority with which they are identified.

Structural analysis enables us to identify the various contexts in which these values and capacities appear, the forms they may take, the objectives they may pursue, and their typical relations with one another within as well as between corporate units. In a structurally homogeneous system based on replication of a single corporate form, the mode of corporate organization will canalize the authority structure and the issues of conflict. It will simultaneously determine the forms of congruence or incongruence between the separate corporate groups. In a structurally heterogeneous system having a variety of corporate forms, we shall also have to look for congruence or incongruence among corporations of differing types, and for interdependence or competition at the various structural levels. Any corporate group embodies a set of structures and procedures which enjoy authority. By definition, all corporations sole are such units. Within, around, and between corporations we shall expect to find recurrent disagreements over alternative courses of action, the interpretation and application of relevant rules, the allocation of positions, privileges and obligations, etc. These issues recurrently develop within the framework of corporate interests, and are settled by direct or indirect exercise of authority and power.

Few serious students now attempt to reduce political systems to the modality of power alone; but many, under Weber's influence, seek to analyze governments solely in terms of authority. Both alternatives are misleading. Our analysis simultaneously stresses the difference and the interdependence of authority and power. The greater the structural simplicity of a given system, that is, its dependence on replication of a single corporate form, such as the Bushman band or Tallensi lineage, the greater its decentralization and the narrower the range in which authority and power may apply. The greater the heterogeneity of corporate types in a given system, the greater the number of levels on which authority and power are simultaneously requisite and manifest, and the more critical their congruence for the integration of the system as a whole.

SIX

ANATOL RAPOPORT
University of Michigan

Some System Approaches
to Political Theory

Like *theory,* the term *system* has both more and less precise meanings; and, as is usual with such multiordinal terms, one pays for precision by a restriction of applicability, and for more general applicability by a loss of precision.

At the outset, let me state one bias, which I share with others of similar philosophical persuasion, concerning definitions. I generally avoid the sort of definition-eliciting question which is put in the form of "What is X?" I usually prefer the form "What can be conveniently or profitably *regarded* as X?" Not "What is a system?" but rather "What sorts of aggregates, portions of the world, conceptual schemes, or whatnot can be conveniently or profitably regarded as systems?" is the question to which various definitions are possible answers.

A fully rigorous definition of *system* would single out from all classes, aggregates, or phenomena those which can satisfy the following criteria:

1. One can specify a set of identifiable elements.
2. Among at least some of the elements, one can specify identifiable relations.
3. Certain relations imply others.

So much constitutes a static system. Dynamics is added by including a time dimension:

> 4. A certain complex of relations at a given time implies a certain complex (or one of several possible complexes) at a later time.

A complete specification of the elements and the relations among them defines a *state* of a system. A dynamic theory of a system is therefore one which enables us to deduce certain future states from a given present state.

It should be noted that this definition places no restrictions on the sort of entities which can be taken as the "elements" of the system. These can be living or nonliving, material or nonmaterial. Nor is any restriction placed on the sort of relations which can obtain among the elements. The only restrictions implied by the requirement of rigor is that both the elements and the relations are unambiguously specifiable. This does not mean that these entities and relations are known as soon as the system is defined. Indeed, the investigation of a system is frequently directed at uncovering the identities of the elements, the nature of the relations, and the dynamic laws governing the behavior or evolution of the system in time.

EXAMPLES

(1) The solar system can be regarded as a system in the sense just defined. The elements are the sun and the planets. The observed relations among them are vectors which specify their relative positions and relative velocities. All of these vectors are, of course, strictly interdependent. The dynamics of this system has been completely worked out. It is, in fact, a deterministic dynamics. Specification of a state at one time completely specifies it (theoretically) for all future and all past times. This nearly complete and exact specification of the system in time was enabled by the discovery of a conceptual scheme known as the Law of Universal Gravitation. On the assumption that the law operates, one can make the calculations which predict and post-dict all the states of the system in time.

It is also noteworthy that at the time of the formulation of the classical theory of the solar system, not all of its elements were known. Some were subsequently discovered by observation, e.g., Uranus, many of the satellites, and the asteroids; two, namely Neptune and Pluto, were deduced by calculations instigated by observed discrepancies between predicted and calculated states. Also, some corrections had to be introduced on the basis of a revised conceptual scheme resulting from the Theory of Relativity. But these discoveries and corrections do not detract from the complete conceptual rigor of the system as it was defined. The theory of the solar system, therefore, remains an outstanding example of an immensely successful system theory. It should be noted also that the success of the theory is directly attributable to its "system" character. Pre-Newtonian theories of celestial mechanics, based on properties of celestial bodies, rather than on relations between them, never achieved the precision and integration which the system theory achieved.

(2) If a gas is enclosed in a container, certain relations obtain among the volume, the pressure, and the temperature of the gas. These relations constitute the static theory of gaseous systems in equilibrium. It is important to note that the entities of that system are not material entities but "state variables"—that is, pressure, volume, and temperature.

It is also possible to view the gas as being composed of material entities, e.g., the molecules of the gas. But in this context, the relations are different: There are now the relative positions and velocities of the particles. If the system is viewed in this way, a deterministic specification of the states is out of the question because of the enormous numbers of entities and relations involved. However, a probabilistic theory has been developed in this context. The statics of the gross (thermodynamic) theory and certain aspects of its dynamics (e.g., the trends toward equilibrium) are derivable from the probabilistic theory.

(3) Systems of chemical reactions single out the concentrations of the various substances as the entities, and the interdependencies among them and their rates of change as the relations.

(4) Ecological systems, mathematically considered, are conceptually quite similar to systems of chemical reactions.

(5) A language is viewed as a system by linguists who single out linguistic entities (phones, phonemes, morphemes, and larger "strings") as the elements, and the rules of their concatenation as the relations. Dynamics is introduced either by considering utterances as time courses of events or, on a larger scale, by considering the evolution of the language.

(6) A kinship system consists of human individuals as elements, and of the kinship relations among them as the relations.

(7) A social system may single out individuals, classes of individuals, social roles, or institutions as its elements, and the functionally important interdependencies among them as the relations.

(8) An international system may view nation-states as the elements, and certain interactions among them as the relations, e.g., alliance, dependence, protectorate, and enemy status.

As we move away from the systems considered in the physical sciences, the conceptualizations become progressively less rigorous, because of the progressively increasing difficulty of operationalizing the relevant concepts. For instance, it may be very well to speak of the population densities and their rates of change in an ecological system, and to note that the equations used to describe the interdependencies of these variables are isomorphic to equations describing a system of chemical reactions. The concentrations and their rates of change in biological systems are much less precisely ascertainable than in chemical systems; also, the laws governing the latter are much more precisely known than the laws governing the former. Thus, while the equations which constitute the mathematical models representing the chemical and the ecological systems may be similar, we have considerably greater confidence in the relevance of the rigor, implied by the equations, to chemical than to ecological systems. Many of the determinants of ecological systems remain unknown, so that the system approach in developing a theory of ecology is more an intellectual commitment than a well-tested methodological tool.

As we move to social systems, even the elements and the relations are ambiguously defined. It may be very well to declare that social roles (rather than, say, individuals) are the concern of some discipline. Arguments of "what is" a social role, or, as some of us would prefer to say, "what should be regarded" as a social role, still comprise the bulk of theoretical discussion. These problems of definition may not be trivial; and it may not be justifiable to deny to them the status of theoretical problems (as many representatives of the "hard" sciences, in their impatience, often do). But one must always keep in mind that this level of theory (problems of definition, categorization, systematization) is far removed from the level at which theory is defined in natural science, namely as collections of logically interdependent and verifiable propositions deduced from a set of explicitly stated assumptions.

So much needs to be said before we broach the subject of the present discussion, the system approach to political theory. As was done previously, we shall understand *theory* both in its stronger and weaker senses. In the stronger sense, a theory must contain logically deduced propositions, which, if referring to portions of the real world, must be in principle verifiable. In its weaker sense, a theory can be simply a preparation of a conceptual scheme in which a theory in the stronger sense will one day be developed. In this sense, a theory is concerned with the singling out of presumably important concepts. If the theory is system-oriented, these concepts will be elements and specifiable relations among those elements. If the theory becomes a theory in the stronger sense, then logically derived and empirically demonstrable relations among the elements will be proposed.

For instance, a system approach to the study of international affairs would, I presume, single out politically organized bodies, e.g., nation-states, as the elements. It would emphasize the relations among the states rather than their inherent characteristics. If these relations are to be shown to be interdependent, then some objective criteria for the existence and the nature of these relations must be proposed. This leads to the problem of designing indices of relations; it may also involve the problem of designing indices for the individual characteristics of nation-states, for it may be the relations among the individual characteristics that in part determine the system relations. The question of finding the "right" indices becomes a crucially important *preliminary* problem of the system approach.

As an example, consider the system of international trade. It is, perhaps, more properly viewed as an economic rather than a political system, but it may be of relevance to political theory. The elements of the system are the trading units, countries, most of which are nation-states. The relations among them are the trade volumes. Now trade volumes obviously depend on the sizes of the corresponding economies. But they may also depend on other factors, such as the political relations among the trading units, transportation facilities, and historical traditions. We can therefore correct for the sizes of the economies by calculating what the imports or exports from one state to another *would have been* had these depended on the sizes of the economies alone. The crude data are thus somewhat refined. The resulting "corrected" figures give us a network of relationships among a set of entities which is indicative of their mutual interactions rather than of their inherent, individual properties.

To ask what can be done with this network is a very pertinent question. The answer is in part provided by the peculiar orientation of the system theorist. For such a theorist, a system is an object of interest in its own right. For example, the network of international trade is, for a system theorist, not so much a map of international trade (which is of obvious interest to the economist) as it is a *network*. Networks have certain system properties. Thus, a network of international trade has certain properties in common with networks of communication, of sociometric choice, of political influence, etc. In some respects, these are similar. In other respects, each has its own distinctive features.

For example, in a network of telephone communications, all the links are symmetric. If an element A can talk over a telephone to element B, so can B talk to A. But in a network of sociometric choices, this is by no means the case. In a recent study of large sociograms, namely the recorded sociometric choices of a group of junior high school students, we found that if A names B as either his best or his next best friend, the chances that B will name A as either his best or his next best friend are only four in ten. Here, then, the links are only partially symmetric. Indeed, we have established a numerical measure of this symmetry, which is a parameter of that particular net. If the links are lines of influence, they can be expected to be "antisymmetric" rather than symmetric. This is strictly true in the case of peck order among hens. If hen A dominates hen B in the peck-order hierarchy, B does not peck A, at least not unless a reversal occurs (which occasionally happens). Thus a peck-order network in a flock of hens will have a mathematical characteristic different from both a network of telephone communication and a network of sociometric choices.

If certain dynamic laws are operating on a system represented by a network, the network will evolve. For example, it is known that the peck-order network characterizing a flock of hens tends to evolve into a complete hierarchy in which all cycles have disappeared. (A cycle is a seemingly anomalous situation in which A pecks B and B pecks C, but C pecks A.)

From this observed trend it is possible to derive or at least to hypothesize some principles of social dynamics which may be underlying the evolution.

The dynamic trends of international trade networks and of large sociogram networks have not been investigated. Their investigation and the concomitant conclusions or hypotheses concerning the underlying dynamics would be the concern of a system theorist. In short, the system theorist centers his attention on the general *system properties*. As he discovers these system properties (static and dynamic), he interprets them in terms of the specific content to which his system refers, or else suggests these interpretations to the specialist concerned with the specific aspects of the system. The specialist can then, perhaps, make more appropriate interpretations in the light of his special experience.

Touching now on the specific topic of this discussion, I should like to mention Lewis Richardson's system approach to international relations.[1] Richardson was concerned with a theory of war. Traditional approaches to this subject centered around concepts developed by historians and other people specifically concerned with international relations: diplomats, politicians, political theorists, and soldiers. Richardson, however, took the system theorist's view. He centered his interest neither on the national interests of specific states, nor on the complex patterns of maneuver and intrigue which have traditionally been considered as the vital content of international relations. Instead, he worked on the implications of a particular hypothesis, namely, that the distrust of one state or bloc of states by another is manifested in hostile acts or acts interpreted as hostile, which, in turn, stimulate the opposite nation or bloc to respond in kind, reinforcing the original trend. This sort of dynamic is now called by cyberneticians "positive feedback." It results in self-catalytic or self-perpetuating processes. It does not take a mathematical argument to show that a system governed by positive feedback will eventually "explode"—that is, the variables characterizing its states will assume infinite values. Accordingly, a mutually reinforcing hostility between rival blocs can be expected to lead to a runaway arms race, and so to war.

A more precise mathematical argument is required if additional factors —e.g., inhibiting effects of costs upon the arms race—are assumed. Here, the system is not unconditionally unstable. The task of mathematical analysis is to deduce the conditions of its stability. Assuming that armament expenditures and volumes of interbloc trade work in opposite directions and postulating certain parameters of restraint, Richardson came to the conclusion that the European international system of 1908–14 was unstable. That is to say, its fate depended on the direction of the initial (slight) impetus which it received from the equilibrium condition. He also derived a remarkable quantitative conclusion, namely, that had the total arms expenditures

[1] L. F. Richardson, *Arms and Insecurity* (Pittsburgh: Boxwood Press, 1960; Chicago: Quadrangle Press, 1960).

in that period been some £5 million less or had the interbloc trade been greater by the same amount, the initial impulse might have been in the opposite direction, toward ever-increasing cooperation (which is also a self-reinforcing process) and so possibly toward a common market and a united Europe.

Now history does not provide us with replicable experiments. We cannot restore the world of 1908 under slightly different conditions to see if the trend could indeed have been reversed. Nor is it useful to draw a lesson in a simple-minded manner from past history, if only because different lessons are sure to be drawn by people with different ideological commitments. There are those who insist that the rise of communism is entirely analogous to the rise of Nazism and that therefore one must destroy it before it is too late. And others feel that the present conflict is more akin to the senseless rivalry of European blocs which led to World War I, or the futile hatred between Catholics and Protestants which devastated Europe in the seventeenth century.

The value of Richardson's work is not in its conclusions, but rather in the suggestiveness of its methodology. The arms-race model is by no means the only one Richardson offered as the underlying dynamic of war. Over a period of thirty years, he made a monumental study of a vast variety of data in an attempt to find significant correlations between various indices characterizing the international system and the incidence of wars. In a way, the search can be regarded as having yielded negative results, for no "critical" index was found. In effect, it remained as unsuccessful as the search for the causes of cancer. Whether it should be abandoned on this ground depends on how important we view the problem to be. Few will advocate the abandonment of the search for the causes of cancer, on which thousands of times more effort has already been spent than on the search for the controllable concomitants of war. Perhaps we can agree that the problem of war also rates a continued expenditure of effort.

Although Richardson's research yielded few if any positive results, it did yield some instructive negative results, in the sense that some cherished notions on the causes of wars were not supported by evidence derived from statistical correlations. In particular, Richardson's own pet theory, which relates wars to preliminary arms races, is corroborated only by the two World Wars and not by earlier historical evidence. It may be, of course, that with the appearance of total war (of which World War I was a near-example), the dynamics of war changed so that arms races now do play a crucial part in the genesis of war. Once more, it must be stressed that not the specific conclusions or hypotheses in Richardson's researches, but rather the indicated methodology is important for building a cogent theory of international relations and war. And Richardson's own methodology was necessarily very crude, because he worked alone and did not have access to modern mathematical technology (high-speed computers).

Given scientific manpower and computing facilities, considerably more could be done. But before I speak of the potentialities of these new developments, let me mention just two results recently obtained, which were directly inspired by Richardson's approach, and more generally, by system orientation.

One study was a follow-up of Richardson's conjecture that there is some characteristic distribution of sizes of groups "organized for aggression." In particular, he noted that the distribution of the sizes (as measured by the number of dead) of bandit raids in Manchukuo in the 1930's exactly paralleled the distribution of sizes of Chicago gangs during the prohibition era. He took the sizes of the raids as indices of the sizes of the raiding bands and conjectured that the similarity of the distributions reflected some "law" governing the formation of human groups organized for aggression.

In a critique of Richardson's work, I had occasion to point out that the conjecture was hardly warranted in view of the fact that the distribution in question (a so-called Yule distribution) was of common occurrence and was observed in a variety of systems with quite disparate contents, e.g., distributions of word frequencies, where "organization for aggression" clearly did not apply.

In the meantime, however, a study made by Coleman and James[2] of "peaceful groups" (specifically groups aggregating around swimming pools) showed that the distributions of sizes of these groups followed a different law, the so-called truncated Poisson distribution. Now the theory of stochastic processes is concerned with deriving distributions from the probabilistic dynamics of a process. It can be shown that the Yule distribution results if the probability that the individual joins a group is proportional to the size of the group, but that no individual leaves the group until the group breaks up. This latter condition, however, is precisely what one would expect in a gang; it is next to impossible for an individual to leave the gang until the gang itself dies. The dynamics leading to the truncated Poisson distribution agrees with the Yule distribution with regard to probability of joining; but leaving the group in this dynamics occurs at random, precisely what one would expect of a casually formed group without binding ties.

Examining the distribution of sizes of war alliances since 1820, we find that they too follow the Yule distribution conjectured by Richardson as characteristic of aggressive aggregates. Moreover, as Horvath and Foster have pointed out, the pairing of the alliances as enemies in wars is explained entirely by chance: There is no evidence that large alliances have a greater tendency to fight large alliances or to gang up against smaller ones.

None of these results are particularly enlightening from the point of view of political theory but they are, I submit, not devoid of interest. The

[2] J. S. Coleman and John James, "The Equilibrium Size Distribution of Freely-Forming Groups," *Sociometry*, XXIV (1961), 36–45.

important thing about them is that the results and conjectures are derived without any reliance on preconceived notions. There can be no question, therefore, of the objectivity of these results. To what extent their relevance to, and significance for, substantive political theory can be increased is something time will tell.

The other study is concerned with the distribution of durations of wars. As is known, Richardson devoted much attention to the distribution of *magnitudes* of wars (defined as a logarithmic measure of the total number of dead), and discovered that this distribution is similar to many other distributions of magnitudes, thus linking his studies to those of Zipf, another early theorist.[3] A recent study by Horvath and Foster of the distribution of durations yields an intriguing result.[4] If we plot durations on a horizontal axis, and plot on the vertical axis the fractions of the total number of wars (from 1820 to the present day) having at least that duration, the resulting curve is approximated by the formula

$$p(t) = e^{-a\sqrt{t}},$$

where $p(t)$ is the fraction of wars having duration at least t, e the base of natural logarithms, and a is a parameter which depends on the time units. Now an empirically oriented investigator would be satisfied that this discovery represented a "law," and, in an earlier day, it would have been announced as such, perhaps christened after its discoverer. But for a system theorist, the relation is a point of departure rather than a point of arrival in an investigation. A system theorist will ask, "What kind of a process is it that would result in such a distribution?"

A minimal acquaintance with probability theory immediately gives at least a rough answer. Suppose the t in the exponent were not under a square-root sign. Then the process would be one which could terminate with equal probability regardless of its duration. Processes of this kind are well-known, e.g., radioactive decay, in which an atom can disintegrate at any moment with equal probability. Now suppose the exponent were a function of t "stronger" than the linear function at—that is, a function whose plot would be convex downward. Such a distribution would result from a process which is the more likely to terminate the longer it lasts. Such processes are also well-known, e.g., human life after a certain age. In the case of the durations of wars, the function in the exponent is "weaker" than at—that is, a function which is convex upward. Such a distribution would result from a process which is the *less* likely to end the longer it lasts. Such processes are also well-known, e.g., lengths of stay in a mental hospital.

The analysis is suggestive. Can it be that wars belong to a class of

[3] G. K. Zipf, *Human Behavior and the Principle of Least Effort* (Cambridge: Addison-Wesley, 1949).

[4] W. J. Horvath and C. C. Foster, "Stochastic Models of War Alliances," *The Journal of Conflict Resolution*, VII (1963), 110–16.

processes which, the longer they last, the harder they are to end? Let us defer the answer until we examine another situation. Horvath and Foster went on to examine the distribution of durations of strikes in a given year in the United States, and found exactly the same relationship except for the value of the time parameter. This would seem to be corroborating evidence, for strikes can be viewed as phenomena belonging to the same class as wars, namely conflicts. Is it true, however, that the longer a strike lasts, the more difficult it is to settle? It would seem that common sense dictates the opposite conclusion because of the hardships, etc. Further analysis makes the originally suggested conclusion unwarranted, for we are dealing not with a single repeated strike but with a whole population of strikes. Some are mild (easy to settle), some severe. It turns out that if the severity of a strike is distributed in a certain reasonable way through the population of strikes, the null hypothesis, namely that a strike is likely to be settled entirely by chance, is tenable. By extension, the same can be said of wars. It seems, therefore, that in the formula representing the statistical distribution of durations, the distribution of severities (be it of wars or of strikes) and the dynamics of the process (whether self-alleviating, self-aggravating, or neutral) are intertwined. Additional investigations are needed in order to disentangle them and so conclude something more definitive about the nature of these processes.

I have had occasion to make such additional investigations in a laboratory experiment involving an experimental game, in which the distribution of durations of so-called "conflict-runs" was observed to follow the same "law." It turned out that after the distribution of parameters (which might have accounted for the distribution of durations) was factored out, a discernible self-perpetuation property of conflict-runs still remained. In that context at least, a self-aggravating property of conflict was apparently demonstrated.

I hope that the foregoing examples give some idea of the flavor of the systems approach. The emphasis is definitely on abstracting from the content of a class of phenomena and of focusing attention on their static and dynamic structures considered as systems in the sense defined, in the hope that the discovery of these structures will shed light on the phenomena in question. Note that this trend is diametrically opposite to a method traditional in the study of history and to some degree in political science. Many historians in our day exert efforts to single out the *unique* features of a historical event. Perhaps this is inevitable in view of the fact that the historian's competence is related to his ability to find out as much as possible about the given event. No detail is irrelevant, because every detail *is* a part of the event, and the "descriptive" historian sees his task as that of *reproducing* the event. In the same way, the biographer, "reproducing" a personality from records, succeeds to the extent that his subject appears as a unique, almost living individual.

Needless to say this method makes theoretical generalizations appear extremely shaky. If every detail is of equal importance, if fingerprints distinguish individuals even better than social status or political roles and for that reason are declared to be important identifying characteristics, then no classification of individuals is relevant; and without classification there can be no social theory. Frequently the historian, and sometimes the political scientist, who has set for himself the task of analyzing unique political events takes pride in his "clinical" approach, sometimes declaring that no generalizations based on analogies can lay claim to validity. Perhaps he is right if by *analogies* we mean the intuitively perceived similarities so common in older speculative theories which, upon closer examination, turned out to be ephemeral. I venture to say, however, that the analogies uncovered by the system approach are of an entirely different sort.

To take an example, the assertion that an automobile eats gasoline can be taken to be purely metaphorical. But in a certain sense it is literally true, because the burning of gasoline liberates energy which propels the car in quite the same way as the oxidation of food liberates energy which activates the muscles.

Comparison of social and political systems to living organisms has been frequently dismissed as metaphorical and naïve. But this is so only if the sole purpose of the comparison is to evoke a suggestive image. If real isomorphisms can be traced between the functioning of living organisms and of political systems (e.g., self-maintenance, growth, evolution) then the comparison is more than allegorical. It carries elements of real "homologies" quite as the analogy between an engine burning fuel and an organism digesting food.

The same holds with regard to the analogies between political and complex physical systems. Only one assumption is needed in order to take these analogies seriously: namely, that *some* degree of determinism is operating in large-scale human affairs. Now arguments about whether there is determinism in human affairs are tedious. Nor can they be resolved without appeals to metaphysical notions, which are accepted or rejected on any but rational grounds. The question is not "whether" but "how much." That some degree of determinism is operating in some aspects of human affairs cannot be denied. No one expects to find the streets of an American city empty of traffic at 5 P.M. on a week day, nor clogged by traffic jams at 5 A.M. on a Sunday. Whatever each of us feels about his inalienable freedom to go or not to go to the bathroom, it is a fact that during the evening hours every half hour on the half hour, when the TV programs change, the water pressure in the mains of every large American city goes down.

Whether mass behavior is a proper subject of study in political theory is a debatable question, but I believe that the opinion that it is, is a respectable one. The French Revolution may have been engineered by the members of the Jacobin Club, and the Russian Revolution by a few intellectuals meeting in the Smolny Institute, but it is unlikely that those revolutions could have happened had the social dynamics in the countries concerned not brought the respective systems (whatever be their nature) into a certain unstable state.

In recent years, one can almost feel the ebb and flow of tension and relaxation in the East-West tug of war. It is foolhardy to predict outcomes on the basis of a few readings. But it seems profitable to give these matters more attention than they had been receiving. Perhaps our interpretation from a system-theoretical point of view will prove enlightening.

The power structures of legislative bodies and of administrative institutions may be partially determined by the structures specifically designed for them (as some political theorists tend to assume), or by the personalities of individuals (as others tend to assume). But the system characteristics of these bodies as determinants of trends (perhaps inexorable trends), of power and influence distribution, and of the concomitant evolution of informal structures should not be neglected either. For example, operationally definable indices of political power have been developed in the theory of n-person games, in which the strategic analysis of coalition formation plays a major part. These indices enable the calculation of power distribution in multiparty legislative bodies and in one-party and two-party bodies, in which formal and informal factions emerge. A system theorist would be interested in the resulting system properties. He might conduct longitudinal studies which might establish predominant secular trends either inherent in the systems themselves or dependent on the initial conditions.

It must be admitted that such studies require an initial sacrifice. Specifically, a political scientist, if he becomes a partisan of the system approach, must usually give up some commitments which have an immediate claim on him as a political scientist. System theory, as we have seen, tends to abstract phenomena from their content and to concentrate on their logical and dynamic structures. This is what we mean when we say that a system is an object of interest per se.

But this is not the first time such sacrifices were demanded in the history of science. The colossal advances in technology were made possible in the beginning of the technological era through a direct preoccupation not with technology but with the heavens, a preoccupation which initiated mechanics as a systematic science. The greatest advances in medicine are traceable not so much to a preoccupation with disease, as to a preoccupation with the world of living things in general, particularly with lowly microbes and mosquitoes, with the dynamics of material transformation, namely chemistry, and with the theory of probability which underlies the mathematics of genetics. Now we know why these things come about. Terrestrial mechanics was advanced by celestial mechanics, because mechanics is of one piece. Human life, health, and disease are all governed by general life phenomena. Hence, if political science is a science of organization, it will advance when general organization theory advances. System theory appears to be an appropriate conceptual framework for studying general principles of organization.

In conclusion, let me return to the role of computing technology which I briefly touched upon earlier. The use of the computer as a simulator has become widespread. Simulation of economic and military systems has become commonplace, and so has the extension of these methods to so-called "diplo-military gaming." Elsewhere, I have sharply criticized the uses to which these methods are put, but their general methodological value cannot be doubted. A simulation is essentially a conceptual experiment (a *gedankenexperiment*) aided by the computer's deductive prowess. It goes without saying that the method of simulation is a system approach. In simulating any process, one simulates a system, because the specification of the simulation program is essentially a specification of the system and its dynamics.

The result of a simulation experiment is essentially the answer to the question, "What would happen if the system under study had such and such structural and dynamic properties?" As has been repeatedly pointed out by serious practitioners of simulation, the greatest value of the method is heuristic. The human participants in a simulation get the feel of the situation to an extent impossible to achieve by verbal descriptions alone. It is the closest thing to participating in the simulated process itself. For particulars, Harold Guetzkow's report of the simulation experiments at Northwestern University is especially recommended.[5]

To summarize, the system approach to political theory amounts to an attempt to theorize about political bodies and political events in terms of precisely specifiable structural and dynamic characteristics. *Precise specifications,* in this context, means neither elegance of formal definition nor finesse of discrimination between shades of meaning; rather, it means an exact indication of how the structural features imply one another and of how the states of the system are determined by previous states. The advantages of this approach are in the opportunities it offers of building political theories which are both general and objectively verifiable. The costs associated with the approach have to do with loss of content-richness and of refinement of conceptualizations with which expertise is usually concerned.

It is precisely those subtle features of political systems and processes whose appreciation marks the expert in the field that must necessarily be absent, at least in the early stages of the gross system approach. It may turn out, however, that the system approach will manifest a richness of its own, which will compensate for the initial impoverishment of content occasioned by it.

---

[5] Harold Guetzkow, *Simulation in International Relations* (Englewood Cliffs, N.J.: Prentice-Hall, Inc., 1963).

SEVEN

DAVID EASTON

University of Chicago

Categories for
*the Systems Analysis of Politics**

The question that gives coherence and purpose to a rigorous analysis of political life as a system of behavior is: How do political systems manage to persist in a world of both stability and change? Ultimately, the search for an answer will reveal what we may call *the life processes of political systems*—those fundamental functions without which no system could endure—together with the typical modes of response through which systems manage to sustain them. The analysis of these processes, and of the nature and conditions of the responses, I posit as a central problem of political theory.

* This essay is a slightly revised version of Chapter Two of my book, *A Systems Analysis of Political Life* (New York: John Wiley & Sons, Inc., 1965). It is reprinted here with permission of the publishers. In effect this essay summarizes my book, *A Framework for Political Analysis* (Englewood Cliffs, N.J.: Prentice-Hall, Inc., 1965) and points forward to the more detailed elaboration of my views now to be found in *A Systems Analysis of Political Life*. The value of its presence here is not only that it offers an overview of the analytic structure developed in both of these volumes, but also that it represents strategy toward a general theory substantially different from the strategies presented in the other essays in this book.

143

POLITICAL LIFE
AS AN OPEN AND ADAPTIVE SYSTEM

Although I shall end by arguing that it is useful to interpret political life as a complex set of processes through which certain kinds of inputs are converted into the type of outputs we may call authoritative policies, decisions, and implementing actions, it is useful at the outset to take a somewhat simpler approach. We may begin by viewing political life as a system of behavior imbedded in an environment to the influences of which the political system itself is exposed and in turn reacts. Several vital considerations are implicit in this interpretation, and it is essential that we become aware of them.

First, such a point of departure for theoretical analysis assumes, without further inquiry, that political interactions in a society constitute a *system* of behavior. This proposition is deceptive in its simplicity. The truth is that if the idea *system* is used with the rigor it permits and with all its currently inherent implications, it provides a starting point that is already heavily freighted with consequences for a whole pattern of analysis.

Second, to the degree that we are successful in analytically isolating political life as a system, it is clear that that system cannot usefully be interpreted as existing in a void. It must be seen as surrounded by physical, biological, social, and psychological *environments*. Here again, the empirical transparency of the statement ought not to distract us from its crucial theoretical significance. If we were to neglect what seems so obvious once it is asserted, it would be impossible to lay the groundwork for an analysis of how political systems manage to persist in a world of stability or change.

This brings us to a third point. What makes the identification of the environments useful and necessary is the further presupposition that political life forms an *open* system. By its very nature as a social system that has been analytically separated from other social systems, such a system must be interpreted as lying exposed to influences deriving from the other systems in which it is embedded. From them flows a constant stream of events and influences that shape the conditions under which the members of the system must act.

Finally, the fact that some systems do survive, whatever the buffets received from their environments, awakens us to the fact that they must have the capacity to *respond* to disturbances and thereby to adapt to the conditions under which they find themselves. Once we are willing to assume that political systems may be adaptive, and need not just react passively to their environmental influences, we shall be able to cut a new path through the complexities of theoretical analysis.

In a political system's internal organization, a critical property that it shares with all other social systems is an extraordinarily variable capacity to respond to the conditions under which it functions. Indeed, political systems accumulate large repertoires of mechanisms by which they may try to cope with their environments. Through these mechanisms, they may regulate their own behavior, transform their internal structure, and even go so far as to remodel their fundamental goals. Few types of systems, other than social systems, have this potentiality. In practice, students of political life cannot help but take this into account; no analysis could even begin to appeal to common sense if it did not do so. Nevertheless, this potentiality is seldom built into a theoretical structure as a central component; certainly its implications for the internal behavior of political systems have never been set forth and explored.[1]

EQUILIBRIUM ANALYSIS AND ITS SHORTCOMINGS

It is a major shortcoming of the one form of inquiry latent but prevalent in political research—equilibrium analysis—that it neglects such variable capacities of systems to cope with environmental influences. Although the equilibrium approach is seldom explicitly elaborated, it has permeated a good part of political research, especially group politics[2] and international relations. Of necessity, an analysis that conceives of a political system as seeking to maintain a state of equilibrium must assume the presence of environmental influences. It is these that displace the power relationships in a political system from their presumed stable state. It is then customary to analyze the system, if only implicitly, in terms of a tendency to return to a presumed pre-existing point of stability. If the system should fail to do so, it would be interpreted as moving on to a new state of equilibrium; and then this would need to be identified and described. A careful scrutiny of the language used reveals that *equilibrium* and *stability* are usually assumed to mean the same thing.[3]

Numerous conceptual and empirical difficulties stand in the way of an effective use of the equilibrium idea for the analysis of political life.[4] Among

[1] K. W. Deutsch, in *The Nerves of Government* (New York: Free Press of Glencoe, Inc., 1963), has considered the consequences of the response capacity of political systems in international affairs, although in very general terms. Some work has also been done for formal organizations. See J. W. Forrester, *Industrial Dynamics* (New York: MIT Press and John Wiley & Sons, Inc., 1961); and W. R. Dill, "The Impact of Environment on Organizational Development," in S. Mailick and E. H. Van Ness, *Concepts and Issues in Administrative Behavior* (Englewood Cliffs, N.J.: Prentice-Hall, Inc., 1962), pp. 94–109.

[2] See David Easton, *The Political System* (New York: Alfred A. Knopf, Inc., 1953) Chapter Eleven.

[3] In "Limits of the Equilibrium Model in Social Research," *Behavioral Science,* I (1956) 96–104, I discuss difficulties created by the fact that social scientists typically fail to distinguish between stability and equilibrium. We often assume that a state of equilibrium must always refer to a stable condition, but in fact there are at least two other kinds of equilibria: neutral and unstable.

[4] Easton, "Limits of the Equilibrium Model."

these difficulties, there are two that are particularly relevant for present purposes.

In the first place, the equilibrium approach leaves the impression that the members of a system have only one basic goal as they seek to cope with change or disturbances: namely, to re-establish the old point of equilibrium or to move on to some new one. This is usually phrased, at least implicitly, as the search for stability, as though stability were sought above all else. In the second place, little if any attention is explicitly given to formulating the problems relating to the path that the system takes in seeking to return to its presumed old point of equilibrium or to attain a new one. It is as though the pathways taken to manage the displacements were an incidental, rather than a central, theoretical consideration.

But it is impossible to understand the processes underlying the capacity of some kind of political life to sustain itself in a society if either the objectives or the form of the responses are taken for granted. A system may well have other goals than that of reaching one or another point of equilibrium. Even though the idea of a state of equilibrium were to be used only as a theoretical norm that is never achieved,[5] such a conception would offer a less useful theoretical approximation of reality than one that takes into account other possibilities. We would find it more helpful to devise a conceptual approach that recognized that members in a system may at times wish to take positive actions to destroy a previous equilibrium or even to achieve some new point of continuing disequilibrium. This is typically the case when the authorities seek to keep themselves in power by fostering internal turmoil or external dangers.

Furthermore, with respect to these variable goals, it is a primary characteristic of all systems that they are able to adopt a wide range of actions of a positive, constructive, and innovative sort for warding off or absorbing any forces of displacement. A system need not react to a disturbance just by oscillating in the neighborhood of a prior point of equilibrium or by shifting to a new one. It may cope with the disturbance by seeking to change its environment so that the exchanges between its environment and itself are no longer stressful; it may seek to insulate itself against any further influences from the environment; or the members of the system may even fundamentally transform their own relationships and modify their own goals and practices so as to improve their chances of handling the inputs from the environment. In these and other ways, a system has the capacity for creative and constructive regulation of disturbances.

It is clear that the adoption of equilibrium analysis, however latent it may be, obscures the presence of system goals that cannot be described as a state of equilibrium. It also virtually conceals the existence of varying

---

[5] J. A. Schumpeter, *Business Cycles* (New York: McGraw-Hill Book Company, 1939), especially in Chapter Two, discusses the idea of equilibrium as a theoretical norm.

pathways for attaining these alternative ends. For any social system, including a political one, adaptation represents more than simple adjustment to the events in its life. It is made up of efforts—limited only by the variety of human skills, resources, and ingenuity—to control, modify, or fundamentally change either the environment or the system itself, or both together. In the outcome, the system may succeed in fending off or incorporating successfully any influences stressful for it.

Minimal Concepts for a Systems Analysis

A systems analysis promises a more expansive, inclusive, and flexible theoretical structure than is available even in a thoroughly self-conscious and well-developed equilibrium approach. To do so successfully, however, a systems analysis must establish its own theoretical imperatives. At the outset, we may define a *system* as any set of variables regardless of the degree of interrelationship among them. The reason for preferring this definition is that it frees us from the need to argue about whether or not a political system is really a system. The only question of importance about a set selected as a system to be analyzed is whether this set constitutes an interesting system. Does it help us to understand and explain some aspect of human behavior of concern to us?

As I have argued in *The Political System,* a *political* system can be designated as those interactions through which values are authoritatively allocated for a society; this is what distinguishes a political system from other systems in its environment. This environment itself may be divided into two parts: the intrasocietal and the extrasocietal. The first consists of those systems in the same society as the political system which are not political systems due to our definition of the nature of political interactions. Intrasocietal systems include such sets of behavior, attitudes, and ideas as the economy, culture, social structure, and personalities; they are functional segments of the society of which the political system is itself a component. In a given society, the systems other than the political system are the source of many influences that create and shape the conditions under which the political system itself must operate. In a world of newly emerging political systems, we do not need to pause to illustrate the impact that a changing economy, culture, or social structure may have upon political life.

The second part of the environment, the extrasocietal, includes all those systems that lie outside the given society itself. They are functional components of an international society, a suprasystem of which any single society is part. The international cultural system is an example of an extrasocietal system.

Taken together, these two classes of systems—the intra- and extrasocietal—which we conceive to lie outside a political system, comprise the *total environment* of a political system.[6] From these sources arise influences that are of consequence for possible stress on the political system. *Disturbances* is a concept that we may use to refer to those influences from the total environment of a system that act upon the system, and thereby change it. Not all disturbances need strain the system: Some may be favorable to the persistence of the system; others may be entirely neutral with regard to stress. But many can be expected to contribute to stress.

When may we say that *stress* occurs? This question involves us in a rather complex idea, one that embodies several subsidiary notions. All political systems as such are distinguished by the fact that if we are to be able to describe them as persisting, we must attribute to them the successful fulfillment of two functions. They must be able to allocate values for a society, and they must manage to induce most members to accept these allocations as binding, at least for most of the time. These two properties distinguish political systems from other kinds of social systems.

Hence, these two distinctive properties—the allocations of values for a society and the relative frequency of compliance with them—are the *essential variables* of political life. But for their presence, we would not be able to say that a society has any political life. And we may here take it for granted that no society could exist without some kind of political system; elsewhere I have sought to demonstrate this in detail.[7]

One of the important reasons for identifying these essential variables is that they give us a way of establishing when and how the disturbances acting upon a system threaten to cause it stress. We can say that stress occurs when there is a danger that the essential variables will be pushed beyond what we may designate as their *critical range*. What this means is that something may be happening in the environment—the system suffers total defeat at the hands of an enemy, or a severe economic crisis arouses widespread disorganization in and disaffection from the system. Let us assume that, as a result, either the authorities are consistently unable to make decisions, or the decisions they do make are no longer regularly accepted as binding. Under these conditions, authoritative allocations of values are no longer possible, and the society collapses for want of a system of behavior to fulfill one of its vital functions.

Here we cannot help but accept the interpretation that the political system had come under stress, so severe that any and every possibility for the persistence of a system for that society had disappeared. But frequently the disruption of a political system is not that complete; even though stress is

---

[6] The total environment is presented in Table 1, Chapter Five, of *A Framework for Political Analysis*. That volume also includes a full discussion of the various components of the environment.

[7] In David Easton, *A Theoretical Approach to Authority*, Office of Naval Research, Technical Report No. 17 (Stanford, California: Department of Economics, 1955).

present, the system continues to persist in some form. Severe as a crisis may be, it still may be possible for the authorities to be able to make some kinds of decisions and to get them accepted with at least minimal frequency, so that some of the problems typically subjected to political settlements can be handled.

In other words, it is not always a matter of whether or not the essential variables are operating. It is possible that they may only be somewhat displaced, as when the authorities are partially unable to make decisions or to get them accepted with complete regularity. Under these circumstances, the essential variables remain within some normal range of operation; they may be under stress, but not to a sufficient degree to displace them beyond a determinable critical point. As long as the system keeps its essential variables operating within their critical range, some kind of system can be said to persist.

As we have seen, every system has the capacity to cope with stress on its essential variables. Not that systems always do so; a system may collapse precisely because it has failed to take measures appropriate for handling the impending stress. But it is the existence of the capacity to respond to stress that is of paramount importance. The kind of response (if any) actually undertaken will help us to evaluate the probability that the system will be able to ward off the stress. Raising the question of the nature of the response to stress points up the special objectives and merit of a systems analysis of political life. It is especially suited for interpreting the behavior of the members in a system in the light of the consequences this behavior has for alleviating or aggravating stress upon the essential variables.

THE LINKAGE VARIABLES BETWEEN SYSTEMS

But a fundamental problem remains: How do the potentially stressful conditions from the environment communicate themselves to a political system? After all, common sense tells us that there is an enormous variety of environmental influences at work on a system. Do we have to treat each change in the environment as a separate and unique disturbance, the specific effects of which have to be independently worked out?

If this were indeed the case, the problems of systematic analysis would be virtually insurmountable. But if we can devise a way for generalizing our method for handling the impact of the environment on the system, there would be some hope of reducing the enormous variety of influences into a manageable number of indicators. This is precisely what I seek to do through the use of the concepts of *inputs* and *outputs*.

How are we to describe these inputs and outputs? Because of the analytic distinction that I have been making between a political system and its parametric or environmental systems, it is useful to interpret the influences associated with the behavior of persons in the environment as *exchanges* or *transactions* that can cross the boundaries of the political system. *Exchanges* will be used when we wish to refer to the mutuality of the relationships between the political system and the other systems in the environment. *Transactions* will be used when we wish to emphasize the movement of an effect in one direction, from an environmental system to the political system, or the reverse, without being concerned at the time about the reactive behavior of the other system.

Up to this point, there is little to dispute. If systems were not in some way coupled together, all analytically identifiable aspects of behavior in society would be independent of each other, a patently unlikely condition. What makes the fact of this coupling more than a mere truism, however, is the proposal of a way to trace out the complex exchanges so that we can readily reduce their immense variety to theoretically and empirically manageable proportions.

To accomplish this, I have proposed that we condense the major and significant environmental influences into a few indicators. Through the examination of these we should be able to appraise and follow through the potential impact of environmental events on the system. With this objective in mind, I have designated the effects that are transmitted across the boundary of a system toward some other system as the outputs of the first system and hence, symmetrically, as the inputs of the second system. A transaction or an exchange between systems will therefore be viewed as a linkage between them in the form of an input-output relationship.

DEMANDS AND SUPPORTS AS INPUT INDICATORS

The value of inputs as a concept is that through their use we shall find it possible to capture the effect of the vast variety of events and conditions in the environment as they pertain to the persistence of a political system. Without using the concept of inputs, it would be difficult to delineate the precise operational way in which the behavior in the various sectors of society affects what happens in the political sphere. Inputs will serve as *summary variables* that concentrate and mirror everything in the environment that is relevant to political stress. Thereby the concept of inputs serves as a powerful analytic tool.

The extent to which inputs can be used as summary variables will depend, however, upon how we define them. We might conceive of them in their broadest sense. In that case, we would interpret them as including any event external to the system that alters, modifies, or affects the system in any way.[8] But if we used the concept in so broad a fashion, we would never be able to exhaust the list of inputs acting upon a system. Virtually every

[8] I am confining my remarks here to external sources of inputs. For the possibility of inputs deriving from internal sources and therefore constituting "withinputs," see *A Framework for Political Analysis*, Chapter Seven.

parametric event and condition would have some significance for the operations of a political system at the focus of attention; a concept so inclusive that it does not help us to organize and simplify reality would defeat its own purposes.

But as I have already intimated, we can greatly simplify the task of analyzing the impact of the environment if we restrict our attention to certain kinds of inputs that can be used as indicators to sum up the most important effects, in terms of their contributions to stress, that cross the boundary from the parametric to the political systems. In this way, we could free ourselves from the need to deal with and trace out separately the consequences of each type of environmental event.

As the theoretical tool for this purpose, it is helpful to view the major environmental influences as focusing in two major inputs: *demands* and *support*. Through them, a wide range of activities in the environment can be channeled, mirrored, summarized, and brought to bear upon political life. Hence, they are key indicators of the way in which environmental influences and conditions modify and shape the operations of the political system. If we wish, we may say that it is through fluctuations in the inputs of demands and support that we shall find the effects of the environmental systems transmitted to the political system.

Outputs and Feedback

In a comparable way, the idea of *outputs* helps us to organize the consequences flowing from the behavior of the members of the system rather than from actions in the environment. Our primary concern is, to be sure, with the functioning of the political system. For understanding political phenomena, we would have no need to be concerned with the consequences in and of themselves that political actions have for the environmental systems. This is a problem that can be better handled by theories dealing with the operations of the economy, culture, or any of the other parametric systems.

But the activities of the members of the system may well have some importance for their own subsequent actions or conditions. To the extent that this is so, we cannot entirely neglect those actions that do flow out of a system into its environment. As in the case of inputs, however, there is an immense amount of activity that takes place within a political system. How are we to isolate the portion relevant to an understanding of the way in which systems manage to persist?

A useful way of simplifying and organizing our perceptions of the behavior of the members of the system (as reflected in their demands and support) is to do so in terms of the effects these inputs have on what we may call the *political outputs*. These are the decisions and actions of the authorities. Not that the complex political processes internal to a system that have been the subject of inquiry for so many decades in political science will be considered in any way irrelevant. Who controls whom in the various decision-making processes will continue to be a vital concern, since the pattern of power relationships helps to determine the nature of the outputs. But the formulation of a conceptual structure for this aspect of a political system would draw us onto a different level of analysis. Here, I am only seeking economical ways of summarizing—not of investigating—the outcomes of these internal political processes, which can, I suggest, be usefully concep-tualized as the outputs of the authorities. Through them, we are able to trace out the consequences of behavior within a political system for its en-vironment.

Outputs not only help to influence events in the broader society of which the system is a part, but also, in doing so, they help to determine each succeeding round of inputs that finds its way into the political system. There is a *feedback loop,* the identification of which helps us to explain the processes through which the system may cope with stress. Through it, the system may take advantage of what has been happening by trying to adjust its future behavior.

When we speak of the system as acting, however, we must be careful not to reify the system itself. We must bear in mind that all systems, to make collective action possible, have those who usually speak in the name or on behalf of the system. We may designate these as the *authorities.* If actions are to be taken to satisfy demands or create conditions that will do so, in-formation must be fed back, at least to these authorities, about the effects of each round of outputs. Without information-feedback about what is hap-pening in the system, the authorities would have to operate in the dark.

If we take as our analytic point of departure the capacity of a system to persist, and if we view as one of the possible and important sources of stress a possible drop in support below some specifiable minimum, we can appreciate the importance of information-feedback to the authorities. The authorities need not necessarily seek to bolster the input of support for themselves or for the system as a whole. But if they should wish to do so—and their own survival may well force them to do so—information about the effects of each round of outputs and about the changing conditions un-der which the members finds themselves is essential. It enables them to take whatever action they feel is necessary to keep support at some minimal level.

For this reason, a model of this kind suggests that exploration of the operations of the feedback processes is of vital significance. Anything that serves to delay, distort, or sever the flow of information to the authorities interferes with their capacity to take action, if so desired, to keep support at a level high enough to ensure the persistence of the system.

The feedback loop itself has a number of parts worthy of detailed in-vestigation. It consists of the production of outputs by the authorities, a response by the members of the society to these outputs, the communication of information about this response to the authorities, and finally, possible succeeding actions by the authorities. Thereby, a new round of outputs, response, information-feedback, and reaction by the authorities is set in motion, forming a seamless web of activities. What happens in this feedback thus has a profound influence on the capacity of a system to cope with stress and persist.

A FLOW MODEL OF THE POLITICAL SYSTEM

It is clear from what has been said that this mode of analysis enables and indeed compels us to analyze a political system in dynamic terms. Not only do we see that a political system gets something done through its outputs, but we are also sensitized to the fact that what the system does may influence each successive stage of behavior. We appreciate the urgent need to interpret political processes as a continuous and interlinked flow of behavior.

If we were to be content with what is basically a static picture of a political system, we might be inclined to stop at this point. Indeed, most political research today does just this. It is concerned with exploring all those intricate subsidiary processes through which decisions are made and put into effect. Therefore, insofar as we were concerned with how influence is used in formulating and putting into effect various kinds of policies or decisions, the model to this point would be an adequate if minimal first approximation.

But the critical problem confronting political theory is not just to develop a conceptual apparatus for understanding the factors that contribute to the kinds of decisions a system makes—that is, to formulate a theory of political allocations. As I have indicated, theory needs to find out how any kind of system manages to persist long enough to continue to make such decisions, and how it deals with the stress to which it may be subjected at any time. For this reason we cannot accept outputs as the terminus of either the political processes or our interest in them. Thus it is important to note, as part of this model, that the outputs of the conversion process characteristically feed back upon the system and thereby shape its subsequent behavior. It is this feature, together with the capacity of a system to take constructive actions, that enables a system to try to adapt or to cope with possible stress.

Thus, a systems analysis of political life rests on the idea of a system imbedded in an environment and subject to possible environmental influences that threaten to drive the essential variables of the system beyond their critical range. Such an analysis suggests that, to persist, the system must be capable of responding with measures that alleviate that stress. The actions of the authorities are particularly critical in this respect. But if they are to be able to respond, they must be in a position to obtain information about what is happening so that they may react insofar as they desire, or are compelled, to do so. With information, they may be able to maintain a minimal level of support for the system.

A systems analysis poses certain major questions, answers to which would help to flesh out the skeletal outline presented here: What precisely is the nature of the influences acting upon a political system? How are they communicated to a system? In what ways, if any, have systems typically sought to cope with such stress? What kinds of feedback processes must exist in any system if it is to acquire and exploit the potential for acting so as to ameliorate these conditions of stress? How do different types of systems —modern or developing, democratic or authoritarian—differ with regard to their types of inputs, outputs, and internal conversion and feedback processes? What effects do these differences have upon the capacity of the system to persist in the face of stress?

The task of theory construction is not of course to give substantive answers to these questions initially. Rather, it is both to formulate the appropriate questions and to devise appropriate ways for seeking answers.⁹

9 I have addressed myself to these objectives in *A Framework for Political Analysis* and *A Systems Analysis of Political Life.*